What Your Colleagues Are Saying . . .

"Feedback is complicated, complex, and layered. *How Feedback Works* made it feel possible and easy! As someone who is familiar with formative assessment practices, which include feedback and peer feedback, I saw the through line immediately. Each module addresses a different type of feedback but also adds a deeper understanding of feedback as new ideas are discussed in various ways. This book added to my own knowledge and pushed me to think a little differently."

—Jeni Mcintyre, Director of Data-Driven Instruction, Tulsa Public Schools

"The contents of this book are accurate, coherent, consistent in theme, and backed up with references and plausible examples. This playbook provides appropriate and relevant guidance for teachers, including learning outcomes and information on misconceptions. It is relevant for all levels of learners in this field—from the lead to the highly accomplished to the proficient and provisional educators."

—Leanne Hebden, Quality Teaching Coach, Literacy, Instructional Leader, Department of Education, Tasmania, Kingston Primary School

"Feedback is the missing link. As educators, we know the important role that feedback plays not just for our students, but for our teaching as well. And yet if we do not understand what that feedback looks like and sounds like, we can never truly know the depth of our impact. *How Feedback Works* gives the teacher the tools they need to know exactly when to use feedback and the kind of feedback that should be given."

—Barbara Lane, San Bernardino County Superintendent of Schools

"Feedback is one of education's most powerful assets in moving learning forward, yet it's often the most misunderstood. *How Feedback Works* ties in pedagogical principles with cognitive science and educational psychology to explain not only how to give effective feedback, but also how to create the structures and conditions necessary for feedback to maximize its potential on student learning. Through explanation, models, and guided practice, this playbook capitalizes on the research to help educators better understand and implement feedback that moves students to and through their next levels of learning. As an educator who coaches teachers, prekindergarten through twelfth grade, I'm excited to have this gem in my back pocket as a relevant reference to share with my colleagues and for developing my own knowledge and skill set around all things feedback."

—Kierstan Barbee, Director of Assessment for Learning

HOW
FEEDBACK WORKS

John Almarode | Douglas Fisher | Nancy Frey

HOW
FEEDBACK WORKS
a playbook

CORWIN
Fisher & Frey

FOR INFORMATION:

Corwin

A SAGE Company

2455 Teller Road

Thousand Oaks, California 91320

(800) 233-9936

www.corwin.com

SAGE Publications Ltd.

1 Oliver's Yard

55 City Road

London EC1Y 1SP

United Kingdom

SAGE Publications India Pvt. Ltd.

B 1/I 1 Mohan Cooperative Industrial Area

Mathura Road, New Delhi 110 044

India

SAGE Publications Asia-Pacific Pte. Ltd.

18 Cross Street #10-10/11/12

China Square Central

Singapore 048423

President: Mike Soules

Vice President and
   Editorial Director: Monica Eckman

Director and Publisher,
   Corwin Classroom: Lisa Luedeke

Associate Content Development
   Editor: Sarah Ross

Editorial Assistant: Nancy Chung

Production Editor: Melanie Birdsall

Typesetter: C&M Digitals (P) Ltd.

Proofreader: Theresa Kay

Indexer: Sheila Hill

Cover Designer: Rose Storey

Marketing Manager: Katie Stoddard

ISBN 978-1-0718-5909-4

Library of Congress Control Number: 2022941920

This book is printed on acid-free paper.

22 23 24 25 26 10 9 8 7 6 5 4 3 2 1

Contents

Visit the companion website at
resources.corwin.com/howfeedbackworks
for more resources.

List of Videos

Note From the Publisher: The authors have provided video and web content throughout the book that is available to you through QR (quick response) codes. To read a QR code, you must have a smartphone or tablet with a camera. We recommend that you download a QR code reader app that is made specifically for your phone or tablet brand.

Videos may also be accessed at **resources.corwin.com/howfeedbackworks**.

Acknowledgments

Corwin gratefully acknowledges the contributions of the following reviewers:

Kierstan Barbee
Director of Assessment for Learning
Dallas, TX

Leanne Hebden
Quality Teaching Coach, Literacy Instructional Leader
Department of Education
Tasmania, Australia

Jeni Mcintyre
Director of Data-Driven Instruction
Tulsa Public Schools
Owasso, OK

Introduction

Dear colleagues,

This is a playbook about feedback. As with all our playbooks, we invite you to learn alongside us as we dive into those strategies, approaches, and influences that research says work best in our schools and classrooms. Playbooks help foster, nurture, and hopefully sustain active engagement with what works best in teaching and learning. This playbook is no different. We are grateful to be learning with you about a well-known but often misunderstood part of the learning process.

Your days, weeks, months, semesters, and years are jammed full of those responsibilities of the job of an educator. With very little downtime, we must ensure that what we do in our schools and classrooms and how we do what we do in our schools and classrooms are both effective and efficient. This includes giving, receiving, and integrating feedback.

> Take a moment to circle, underline, and/or highlight the words *giving, receiving,* and *integrating* mentioned in the previous sentence. These three words will appear over and over again as we embark on this learning journey. While the importance of these three words may not be clear this early on in our journey, by the time you read the last sentence in this playbook, you'll find that these three words will guide you as you apply your learning to your own school or classroom.

In fact, for us, feedback is the one area that *can* cause the greatest strain on us as educators. While we may acknowledge and believe that feedback is an important and essential part of the learning process, we are confronted with challenges of feedback in our own classrooms. Maybe you can relate to the following questions, which are always on our minds:

1. When we have a full classroom of students and a variety of assignments and tasks, how can we possibly ensure that all of them get the feedback they need?

2. What type of feedback is most helpful in learning? Simply telling students that a particular response or action is not correct cannot be enough, right?

3. How do we get our students to receive the feedback and edit, revise, or change their approach the next time? What if our students simply toss the feedback in the book, desk, backpack, or, even worse, the trashcan?

4. What role do our students play in giving and receiving feedback? After all, they will not be in our classrooms forever and will have to transition to independent learners.

Could you hear yourself or your colleagues asking these same questions? Could you relate to each of the above four concerns about feedback? These questions and concerns are what lead us to actively engage with the question, *how does feedback work?*

What additional questions or concerns do you have about feedback? Write them out in the space below so that we can revisit them throughout our work in this playbook.

If feedback is such an important and essential part of the learning process, we must uncover how to implement effective feedback effectively and efficiently in our schools and classrooms. Ignoring this important and essential part of the learning process will impede the learning progress of our students. That is something none of us wants to do.

Each of the modules in this playbook has a specific focus on understanding *how feedback works* and how to make feedback work in your unique school and classroom. We will be explicit about our focus within each module by providing a learning intention and desired outcomes. Moving from research to reality, each module will look at a specific aspect of feedback and provide examples and opportunities for you to apply that specific aspect to your school or classroom.

Part I of this playbook will set the foundation for giving, receiving, and integrating feedback. These first five modules will help us develop a definition of feedback, explore the latest research on feedback, identify barriers to giving, receiving, and integrating feedback, and introduce the four foundational elements to high-quality, high-impact feedback. One by one, we will spend the remaining modules in the playbook taking a deep dive into each of the four foundational elements that make feedback work. To support the learning of these, we call these foundational elements the **Four Cs of Feedback**. Be patient; we will introduce those to you very soon.

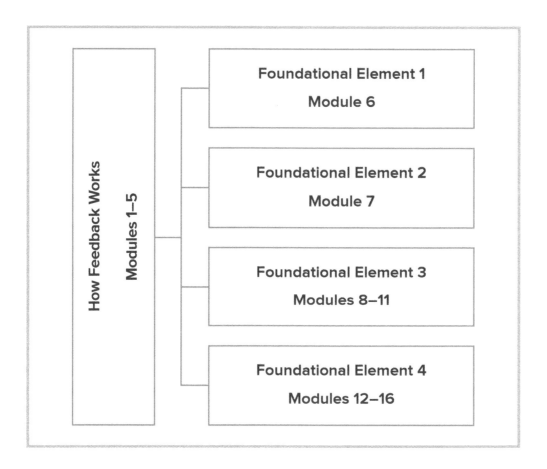

Throughout the pages of this playbook, we strive to include examples from primary, elementary, middle school, and high school content, skills, practices, dispositions, and understandings. From building a case for the reduction of fossil fuels to analyzing primary sources in history to creating a still-life painting, feedback is essential to advancing learning. But we should not go at this alone—which is why we are joining you on this learning journey. Who will you collaborate with to uncover how feedback works?

COLLABORATING FOR GREAT LEARNING

Each module offers you an opportunity for practice and application with a variety of grade levels and content areas. We encourage you to engage in this playbook by circling, highlighting, underlining, writing your own notes and responses, and using sticky notes to mark pages. Most importantly, though, we encourage you to collaborate with your colleagues on this journey. Although using this playbook as part of your personal learning is fine, the opportunity to dialogue about *how feedback works* and collaborate on how to make it work in our school and classroom is best done collectively with colleagues. We offer three suggestions for collaborating with another to use this playbook:

- ➡ With an accountability partner
- ➡ With an instructional coach
- ➡ During your common planning or PLC+ meeting (see Fisher et al., 2020)

Let's start with accountability partners. The use of this playbook during common planning or your PLC+ meeting may not be feasible. You may be more comfortable partnering with a colleague across the hall, in another part of the building, or in another school. You and this colleague can move through the modules, engage in the tasks, implement ideas in your own classrooms, and debrief the impact this had on advancing student learning. You and this colleague will serve as accountability partners in increasing your understanding of *how feedback works* and leveraging your new learning in the design of your classrooms, learning experiences, and tasks.

A second way to work collaboratively through this playbook is to work alongside an instructional coach. Instructional coaches provide all of us with an outside perspective on the teaching and learning in our classrooms. They can provide us with the right feedback at the right time. In fact, working with an instructional coach may offer the opportunity for the instructional coach to build their capacity by applying *how feedback works* to the instructional coaching cycle. Either way, sitting down with an instructional coach, engaging in critical dialogue about *how feedback works*, designing experiences and tasks, and then working together to evaluate the impact on student learning is an invaluable asset to professional growth.

Finally, this playbook can support collaborative conversations during your PLC+ meeting (Fisher et al., 2020). The work of this playbook is another tool for the work you do in your PLC+. The use of these five guiding questions of PLC+ will keep the focus relentlessly on the learning of our students:

- ➡ Where are we going?
- ➡ Where are we now?
- ➡ How do we move learning forward?
- ➡ What did we learn today?
- ➡ Who benefited and who did not benefit? (Fisher et al., 2020, pp. 8–9)

In PLC+, teachers identify learning intentions and discuss ideas for instruction. They meet to review student work and figure out if their efforts have been fruitful. They also talk about students who need additional instruction or support for success (see the following table). To revisit an earlier idea, understanding *how feedback works* is essential in navigating the implementation of effective feedback and advancing learning. This is best done together, during our work as a community of learners.

HOW THIS PLAYBOOK SUPPORTS THE WORK OF PLC+

PLC Question	Module
Where are we going?	The nature of the feedback given and received tells us where additional teaching and learning are necessary. This requires that we maintain clarity about the learning. **Modules 1–5, 8, 9**
Where are we now?	Noticing where our learners are in the progression and the generation of evidence to make teaching and learning visible tells us where we are now. **Modules 9, 10**
How do we move learning forward?	Moving learning forward requires the giving, receiving, and integrating of feedback. We, alongside our learners, must engage in the feedback loop, remove the barriers to the exchanging of feedback, and effectively communicate that feedback. **Modules 3, 5–7, 11–16**
What did we learn today?	Having a clear understanding of what we learned today (both us and our learners) requires noticing what learners are saying and doing and communicating with them around their learning. **Modules 8–10, 15, 16**
Who benefited and who did not benefit?	While every module of this playbook applies to this particular question, the primary module is around noticing which learners are giving, receiving, and integrating feedback. If we do not take notice of how learners are engaging with feedback, we will never know if they are benefiting from feedback. **Modules 9, 10**

Whether you have an accountability partner, access to an instructional coach, or a high-functioning, high-impact PLC+, the benefit of a collaborative approach is the opportunity to engage in critical dialogue around what learning looks like for you and your learners.

This brings us to the singular focus of this playbook. Together, we will take an up-close look at feedback in our schools and classrooms. By the time we arrive at the final pages of this playbook, we will be able to answer the essential question

How does feedback work?

and apply that answer to our schools and classrooms. Again, we are glad you are here to learn alongside us in this playbook.

Sincerely,

John, Doug, and Nancy

Video I.1: Introduction to *How Feedback Works: A Playbook*
resources.corwin.com/howfeedbackworks

To read a QR code, you must have a smartphone or tablet with a camera. We recommend that you download a QR code reader app that is made specifically for your phone or tablet brand.

PART I

SETTING THE FOUNDATION FOR HOW FEEDBACK WORKS

In this section:

1

WHAT IS FEEDBACK?

LEARNING INTENTION

In this module, we are learning the definition of feedback so that we can better understand what feedback looks like in our schools and classrooms.

SUCCESS CRITERIA

We have successfully completed this module when

1. We can define feedback in our own words.

2. We can connect the definition of feedback with specific actions in our schools and classrooms.

3. We can identify specific examples of when feedback works in our schools and classrooms.

Video 1.1: Introduction to Module 1
resources.corwin.com/howfeedbackworks

Feedback is an essential part of the learning process. As classroom teachers, we constantly seek feedback to gain a sense of how our learners are progressing in the learning experience or task. From a much larger perspective, we seek feedback to gain an understanding of how learners are progressing toward the overall learning goals or targets for the academic semester or year. On the other side of the desk, our learners seek feedback to know if they are headed in the right direction in learning content, skills, and understandings.

However, each of us has our own understanding of what feedback is, what feedback looks like, and the ways to seek feedback. Use the space provided on the next page to jot down your prior knowledge and prior experiences with feedback. What is your understanding of *how feedback works*?

What do you currently see in your own school and classroom that you would identify or classify as feedback?	
What do you think feedback should look like in order to move learning forward?	
What are the different ways you currently seek feedback to gain a sense of how your learners are progressing?	

Again, feedback is an essential part of the learning process. Now that you have shared your current thinking, let's begin to explore the importance of feedback with an example from the toy section at your local department store.

Building blocks, puzzles, and furniture shine a spotlight on the value of feedback. Whether using blocks to make a model airplane, working on a 1,000-piece landscape puzzle, or putting together a bookshelf you just purchased for your classroom, monitoring your *progress* throughout the *process* ensures that you don't arrive at the end of your task with misaligned wings, a puzzle that doesn't match the picture on the box, or a crocked bookshelf (not to mention the dread of having extra pieces and parts lying around). Using the idea that feedback helps us gain a sense of *progress*, use the space provided to list all the ways you and your colleagues might monitor your *process* in building with blocks, completing a puzzle, or putting together a bookshelf. You don't have to do all three, but be very specific with the one you and your colleagues select. We provided two examples for the puzzle task to get you started.

	What You Need to Do to Monitor the Process	Questions You Would Ask Yourself or Others From Whom You Need Feedback
Building a Block Airplane		
Completing a Puzzle	*Example:* • **Look at the picture on the box to see the finished product.** • **Arrange the pieces into piles with similar coloring.**	
Putting Together a Bookshelf		

This is certainly not a playbook about blocks, puzzles, and furniture. So, now let's replace the three tasks above with the following:

1. Instead of building an airplane, what if learners were asked to build a case for the reduction of fossil fuel use for a high school environmental science class?

2. Instead of completing a puzzle, what if learners were asked to complete an analysis of primary sources to make informed judgments about a particular historical event?

3. Instead of putting together a bookshelf, what if learners were asked to put together the elements of color, value, patterns, and emphasis to create a still-life painting?

It turns out that monitoring the *progress* throughout the *process* of each of the revised tasks is an essential part of the overall learning process. Using your responses from the previous task, revise them to reflect the science, social studies, and/or art task. An example is provided for you.

Building a Case for Fossil Fuel Reduction	Completing an Analysis of Primary Sources	Creating a Still-Life Painting
	Instead of . . . Look at the picture on the box to see the finished product . . . • **Try . . .** Look at an exemplar response to see what a successful analysis looks like. **Instead of . . .** Arrange the pieces into piles with similar coloring . . . • **Try . . .** Highlight specific parts of the document with different colors based on similar information.	

You and your colleagues may have noticed that revising your responses to the first task (i.e., building blocks, puzzles, and furniture) to fit a science, social studies, and/or art task was easier than expected. With very minor edits, the same ways you and your colleagues might monitor your *progress* and *process* in building a plane, completing a puzzle, or putting together a bookshelf applies to science, social studies, and art. This strongly suggests that there is a common set of features in all feedback that makes feedback essential and important. Similarly, if this common feature or set of features is missing, the feedback loses power in the process. For example, if you and your colleagues had simply responded to the previous tasks by stating you would stand by and keep saying, "try harder, keep at it, you can do it," little progress would be made in any of these tasks. So, what is the common set of features that make feedback essential and important?

Before moving forward, take a moment to discuss what you and your colleagues believe are the common features that make feedback essential and important to the learning process. In other words, what makes your feedback effective?

Keep this page marked. We will come back and revise your initial response. For now, let's unpack the definition of feedback.

THE DEFINITION OF FEEDBACK

The very definition of feedback provides an on-ramp to identify the features of effective feedback. Using your phone, tablet, computer, or a good-ol'-fashioned dictionary, look up the definition of *feedback* and write all parts of the definition that stand out to you in the box below.

What is the official definition of *feedback*?

We used Merriam-Webster's online dictionary to pull down the official definition:

1. a. the transmission of evaluative or corrective information about an action, event, or process to the original or controlling source also: the information so transmitted

    b. the partial reversion of the effects of a process to its source or to a preceding stage;

2. the return to the input of a part of the output of a machine, system, or process (as for producing changes in an electronic circuit that improve performance or in an automatic control device that provides self-corrective action)

3. a rumbling, whining, or whistling sound resulting from an amplified or broadcast signal (such as music or speech) that has been returned as input and retransmitted. (Merriam-Webster, 2021)

There are several key words contained in Merriam-Webster's definition of *feedback* that will guide our learning in the subsequent modules of this playbook. For now, circle, highlight, or underline the following words from above.

> From part 1 a, **corrective information**
>
> From part 1 a, **process**
>
> From part 2, **output**
>
> From part 2, **improve performance**
>
> From part 3, **returned as input**

These key words, extracted from the general definition of feedback, provide the foundation for understanding the definition of feedback and *how feedback works* in our classrooms. Take a moment to construct your own definition of feedback in your classroom. Edit and revise the official definition to contextualize what is meant by feedback in our schools and classrooms. Write that definition below.

A contextualized definition of *feedback* is . . .

Now, let's apply your own definition of feedback to the teaching and learning in your classroom. Use the space provided to describe what each aspect of the definition of feedback would look like in your classroom. We have provided examples to get you started.

Aspects of the Definition of Feedback	Our Example	What This Looks Like in My Classroom
Corrective Information	Students are provided comments highlighting aspects that need revising in their narrative essays.	
Process	Students conference with a peer to integrate the feedback to make revisions to the narrative essay.	
Output	Students individually prepare the next draft of their narrative essays.	
Improved Performance	Students once again conference with a peer to compare and contrast the drafts of their narrative essays.	
Returned as Input	Students resubmit their narrative essays. This is input for us, as teachers, to get feedback on both peer conferencing and the writing process.	

Now that we have developed a definition of feedback and begun to connect that to our teaching and learning, we turn our attention to what the research says about *how feedback works*.

Take a moment to reflect on your learning. How are you progressing? Where do you need to spend a little more time in this module?

Consider these questions to guide your self-reflection and self-assessment:

1. Can I define *feedback* in our own words?

2. Can I connect the definition of feedback with specific actions in our schools and classrooms?

3. Can I identify specific examples of when feedback works in our schools and classrooms?

Access videos and other resources at
resources.corwin.com/howfeedbackworks.

WHAT DOES THE LATEST RESEARCH SAY ABOUT FEEDBACK?

LEARNING INTENTION

Now we are learning about the latest research on feedback so that we can understand the different aspects of how feedback works.

SUCCESS CRITERIA

We have successfully completed this module when

1. We can summarize the latest findings from the research on feedback.

2. We can identify the major takeaways that are applicable to teaching and learning.

UNPACKING THE RESEARCH

Research has long supported the opening sentence of Module 1: *Feedback is an essential part of the learning process.* Effective feedback has the potential to advance learning in our schools and classrooms. For example, in 2009, John Hattie identified 23 meta-analyses, composed of 1,287 studies looking at the influence of feedback on student learning. The average effect size of this compilation of research was found to be 0.73 (Hattie, 2009). But what does this mean?

An effect size is a way to quantify the magnitude of a particular influence on a specific outcome. In the case of feedback and the 23 meta-analyses mentioned above, the specific outcome is student learning. Therefore, an effect size of 0.73 is the magnitude of feedback on student learning. The number, 0.73, refers to the number of standard

Video 2.1: Introduction to Module 2

resources.corwin.com/ howfeedbackworks

deviations of growth associated with feedback and provides insight into how strong a particular influence is when compared to other influences on student learning (bullying, one-to-one laptops, classroom discussion, homework, etc.). In 2009, the research showed that feedback was well above the average effect size of influences on student learning and had the potential to almost double the rate of learning in our schools and classrooms.

Before moving on, take a moment to summarize the concept of effect size and what insight an effect size provides in teaching and learning. You can certainly pull from other sources to summarize your thinking.

However, there is more to the story. Since 2009, there has been a change in the research around feedback in schools and classrooms. For example, in 2022 there are now 7 meta-analyses and 798 studies. Did you see it? Yep, we caught that apparent discrepancy as well. How can we go from 2009 to 2022 and see a drop in meta-analyses and studies? Those meta-analyses and studies didn't just disappear, right? That is the new part of the story and the part we will unpack in this playbook. What does the research now say about feedback?

Since 2009, research on feedback has looked beyond this potentially powerful influence as a single construct and more toward a multi-dimensional aspect of the learning process in our schools and classrooms. Since 2009, we have learned more about *how feedback works.*

What does the research *now* say about feedback?

1. Visit www.visiblelearningmetax.com. You will probably want to explore this website and get a sense of the information contained within the pages of this URL.

2. When ready, select **Teaching Strategies**, the section with the orange border containing those factors or influences related to learning intentions, success criteria, and, you guessed it, feedback.

3. Scroll down and locate **feedback** in the list of influences. What do you notice about **feedback** and how this particular influence is listed in Meta[X]?

4. Using the following chart, let's capture this new aspect of the research on feedback. We will do the first one for you, related to the overall effect of feedback.

Video 2.2: Meta[X] and Feedback

resources.corwin.com/ howfeedbackworks

Influence Related to Feedback	Potential Impact on Student Learning	Summary of What This Means to Me	Other Things I Noticed and Want to Remember
Feedback (In General)	Potential to considerably accelerate	Feedback in the classroom can be defined as "information allowing a learner to reduce the gap between what is evident currently and what could or should be the case."	The effect size is 0.62—why the decrease? What does this mean?
Cues and Reinforcements			
Feedback With Technology			

(Continued)

(Continued)

Influence Related to Feedback	Potential Impact on Student Learning	Summary of What This Means to Me	Other Things I Noticed and Want to Remember

Video 2.3: Meta^X and Visible Learning
resources.corwin.com/
howfeedbackworks

As we have mentioned earlier, the research on feedback has changed since 2009. In fact, the overall effect size has decreased from 0.73 (Hattie, 2009) to 0.62 (Visible Learning Meta^X, 2022). Why the decrease? What does this mean? Our hope is that your work in the previous task will begin to answer both of those questions. First and foremost, there is no doubt that feedback is an essential part of teaching and learning. What the now 37 meta-analyses, composed of 1,620 studies, say about feedback is this:

1. Feedback is multi-dimensional and cannot be treated as a one-dimensional concept.

2. There are now previously unstudied and different aspects to feedback (reinforcement and cues, self, technology, timing, etc.) and having a singular view of feedback is not sufficient in advancing learning in our schools and classrooms.

3. There is a lot of variation in each dimension of feedback. For example, reinforcement and cues have an average effect size of 0.92, while self-feedback has an average effect size of 0.13. This variation is important and must be explored in greater detail.

4. And finally, understanding *how feedback works* is essential in navigating the implementation of effective feedback and advancing learning in our schools and classrooms.

WHERE TO NEXT?

We have started strong in this playbook! Together we have

➜ Looked at the value and role of feedback in our *progress* through any *process* (i.e., putting together blocks, a puzzle, a bookshelf, or doing science, social studies, and art projects).

➜ Looked at the official definition of feedback to gain insight into how this powerful influence on learning might work in our schools and classrooms.

➜ Taken a giant step into the research around feedback and how this research has changed over the past several decades.

Now the real work begins. As we close out this module and move into the next module, we will shift our focus from *what* to *how*. Take a moment to refer to the fourth takeaway on page 20. To emphasize where we are going next, please rewrite that takeaway below in the box. Yes, we are really asking you to copy the fourth takeaway into the below box: this is the core purpose of our work moving forward in this playbook.

> Understanding . . .

Before moving into Module 3, let's do a quick learning check. This strategy is called T–P–E (adapted from Ritchhart et al., 2011). In addition to supporting our learning in this playbook, the T–P–E strategy plays a role in effective feedback. That role is the focus of Module 3. But first, use the space on the following pages to check on your own learning from these first two modules.

T (Think): What thoughts do you have about feedback after completing these first modules? What do these ideas and tasks have you thinking about with regard to feedback?

P (Puzzle): What puzzles you about feedback? After digging into these first few modules, what puzzles you about the concepts associated with feedback?

E (Explore): What questions do you want to have answered by the time you and your colleagues finish the final module of this playbook? What are you hoping to get out of this learning journey? State those expectations in the form of three or four questions.

Take a moment to reflect on your learning. How are you progressing? Where do you need to spend a little more time in this module?

Consider these questions to guide your self-reflection and self-assessment:

1. Can I summarize the latest findings from the research on feedback?

2. Can I identify the major takeaways that are applicable to teaching and learning?

 online resources

Access videos and other resources at
resources.corwin.com/howfeedbackworks.

WHAT DOES THE FEEDBACK PROCESS LOOK LIKE IN ACTION?

LEARNING INTENTION

In this module, we are learning about the three aspects of feedback and how they operate as a continuous loop.

SUCCESS CRITERIA

We have successfully completed this module when

1. I can explain the three aspects of feedback.

2. I can describe what is meant by "feedback as a continuous loop."

3. I can list the three questions most commonly associated with how feedback works.

Video 3.1: Introduction to Module 3
resources.corwin.com/howfeedbackworks

Up to this point, we have developed a working definition of feedback and begun unpacking the complex body of research around *how feedback works*. As we move a step closer to translating the research to reality in our schools and classrooms, let's start chipping away at our guiding question for this playbook, *how does feedback work*?

Flip back to Module 1, page 9, where you were asked to describe how you think feedback works. Reread your answers or responses to those questions. With a highlighter or other writing instrument, mark the number of times you referenced the **teacher as the source of the feedback**.

If you are like us, our initial responses to *how feedback works* focused on us, the teacher, as the primary source of feedback. Carrying the full weight of feedback on our shoulders likely leads directly to our concern about feedback. Do you remember the questions posed in the Introduction of this playbook?

1. When we have a full classroom of students and a variety of assignments and tasks, how can we possibly ensure that all of them get the feedback they need?

2. What type of feedback is most helpful in learning? Simply telling students that a particular response or action is not correct cannot be enough, right?

3. How do we get our students to receive the feedback and edit, revise, or change their approach the next time? What if our students simply toss the feedback in the book, desk, backpack, or, even worse, the trashcan?

4. What role do our students play in giving and receiving feedback? After all, they will not be in our classrooms forever and will have to transition to independent learners.

The uncertainty communicated in these questions is likely due to the belief that we are the only source of feedback in our schools and classrooms. We want to tackle that belief in this module.

Let's start with a story. John's father is a bluegrass musician. He has been playing music since he was a child and has been blessed with opportunities to travel and record multiple albums. As a child, John would travel with his father and sit in on the necessary sound checks prior to a show. What John most vividly recalls about those sound checks was the frequent loud, painful, and high-pitched squeal caused by microphone feedback. The purpose of sound checks was to set up the soundboard and microphones to maximize the experience for those audience members that had traveled to hear high-quality bluegrass music.

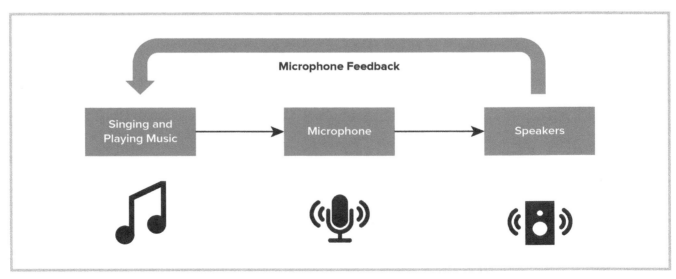

Image source: iStock.com/-VICTOR-

Microphone feedback happens when the sound from the speakers is picked up by the microphone. In fact, this is the third part of the official definition of feedback presented on page 13 in Module 1.

3.   a rumbling, whining, or whistling sound resulting from an amplified or broadcast signal (such as music or speech) that has been returned as input and retransmitted. (Merriam-Webster, 2021)

You likely have experienced microphone feedback in your school's auditorium, cafeteria, or intercom system. Whether at a sound check with John's father or in your own school, microphone feedback prompts an immediate and rapid response from everyone within ear-shot of the feedback. For example, the person speaking into the microphone pulls back from the microphone and may even stop speaking. The audience members stop what they are doing and turn their attention to the source of the feedback. Finally, there is likely an adjustment made to the controls of the soundboard (e.g., the volume, sensitivity). The nature of each of these actions is in direct response to the microphone feedback. While sound checks aim to reduce the number of adjustments needed, there are so many variables at play that the adjustments made by the speaker and the person running the soundboard continuously happen through this dynamic feedback loop.

This is exactly how feedback in our schools and classrooms works. Use the diagram below to connect the concept of microphone feedback with feedback in our schools and classrooms. Refer to the microphone feedback diagram on page 25. Where would the (1) teacher, (2) the learning experience, (3) the student, and (4) feedback go in this diagram?

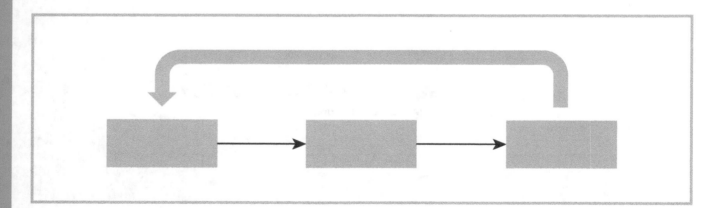

After you have completed the above diagram, please use the following questions to continue to connect microphone feedback with feedback in our schools and classrooms. Use the space after each question to record the thinking of you and your colleagues.

1. How is the squeal of microphone feedback similar to what happens in our schools and classrooms?

2. Which aspect of this analogy is most like our students?

3. Which aspect of this analogy is most like us, as teachers?

4. How are the actions of the "musicians" and individuals running the soundboard similar to us and our students in the classroom?

5. What is analogous to "high-quality music" in our schools and classrooms?

The musician and the microphone feedback analogy helps us see that:

➡ There are three aspects to feedback: giving, receiving, and adjusting.

➡ These three aspects interact through a continuous and dynamic feedback loop.

THREE ASPECTS OF FEEDBACK

For feedback to work and be effective in monitoring the *progress* throughout the *process*, three aspects must always be present.

1. There must be a source of feedback that transmits corrective information about an action, event, or process. Take a look back at Merriam-Webster's definition of feedback on page 13 in Module 1 of this playbook. This is what we refer to as the **Giver of the Feedback**.

2. There must be a **Receiver of the Feedback**. The feedback must be received by the individual or individuals that are engaged in the action, event, or process.

3. And finally, the receiver of the feedback must **Integrate the Feedback** into their decisions about where to go next in the progress through the process. The feedback is effective when the receiver of the feedback takes the corrective information transmitted by the giver and adjusts their progress through the process.

Use the space below to reflect on the three aspects of feedback. You can summarize your thinking or reflect on the idea that effective feedback requires a giver, receiver, and integration. What does that mean to you and your colleagues?

When we look at feedback through this multidimensional lens, we now expand our understanding of *how feedback works*. This expanded view comes from the fact that there are now multiple givers and receivers in our schools and classrooms. Notice that the three aspects are not attached to a specific individual. The giver is any individual or thing that provides corrective information. Likewise, the receiver is not limited to our learners. We are receivers as well, and we must integrate the feedback coming from learners into decisions about where to go next in our progress through the process of teaching. This statement is very important. For emphasis, fill in the missing parts of words below for this important idea.

I, as a teacher, am a rec_____ of feedback as well, and must int_____

the feedback coming from my lea_____ into decisions about where to go next in

my tea_____.

Finally, if teachers, learners, and other mechanisms can give feedback *and* both teachers and learners are receivers of feedback, then both teachers and learners are integrating and making adjustments for feedback to work.

FEEDBACK IS A CONTINUOUS LOOP

There is a very important statement we want to return to on page 26 in this module. To help us out, the statement is provided in the box below.

> While sound checks aim to reduce the number of adjustments needed, there are so many variables at play that the adjustments made by the speaker and the person running the soundboard continuously happen through this dynamic feedback loop.

Feedback works when there is continuous giving, receiving, and integrating during the learning process. Sound checks only take musicians so far in the preparation for the show. Once the auditorium, concert hall, or arena is full of audience members, continuous adjustments must be made based on the response of the crowd. Furthermore, changes in the weather (e.g., humidity) will have an impact on the sound. Musicians are also known for "going off script" and adding different elements or aspects to the performance in response to the audiences' reactions. This adds another variable that may require adjustments to the soundboard. Feedback is not a single event or something that has an end. Feedback is a continuous and dynamic loop driven by the giving, receiving, and integrating of feedback.

A way to think about the feedback loop is to think in terms of *feed-up, feed-back,* and *feed-forward.*

Feedback is a continuous and dynamic loop driven by the giving, receiving, and integrating of feedback.

 **Feed-Up**

The part of the feedback loop that establishes the intention and criteria for success associated with process and/or product. At this point in the feedback loop, we are seeking to establish and communicate purpose, while at the same time ensuring that all stakeholders understand how the process and product will be assessed.

Feed-Up Answers the Question *Where are we going?*

For the musicians in our example, this would be the performance standards or expectations they have established and communicated with the soundboard operator. In other words, what do they want their music to sound like while they are live and on the stage? This must be communicated to the soundboard operator in the form of feed-up. Similarly, audience members arrive at the performance with prior knowledge and beliefs about what the music should and will sound like—this is communicated through their responses and reactions to musicians.

How do you and your colleagues already engage in *feed-up*? List specific strategies, practices, or examples in the space provided. We will come back to this later on in our work through the playbook.

 Feed-Back

This part of the loop occurs during the process and development of the product. Feed-back provides vital information about how things are progressing toward the intention and criteria for success established in feed-up. At this stage of the feedback loop, all the stakeholders are getting information that helps them to understand how they are doing in the process toward the product.

This particular part of the loop is identified as feed-*back* because both the giver and the receiver of the feedback must look back at the intention and criteria for success to understand where they are relative to that intention or the criteria for success.

Feed-Back Answers the Question *Where are we now?*

For the musicians and audience members, this is done during the concert and involves listening for changes in the performance or sound quality. The musicians may adjust their positions relative to the microphone, the volume of their voices, or the way they play their instruments. The sound engineer, the individual running the soundboard, may make minor adjustments to the balance of the microphones, alter the high or low sounds, or provide built-in effects such as echo or reverb for the musicians. And, as you might suspect, the audience members, through their cheers or jeers, communicate how well the performance is going.

How do you and your colleagues already engage in *feed-back*? List specific strategies, practices, or examples in the space provided. We will come back to this later on in our work through the playbook.

〉〉〉 Feed-Forward

Quite arguably, the most important part of the feedback loop is what is done with the information generated for feed-back. In other words, the information we now have about how our learners are doing in the process toward the product should inform what we do next and where we go next in the learning experience. Feed-*forward* places value on both the feed-up and feed-back parts of the continuous loop by adjusting future experiences to improve learning.

Using the space below, write down why you believe that *feed-forward* is an essential part of the teaching and learning process. Why would this part of the loop be called *feed-forward*?

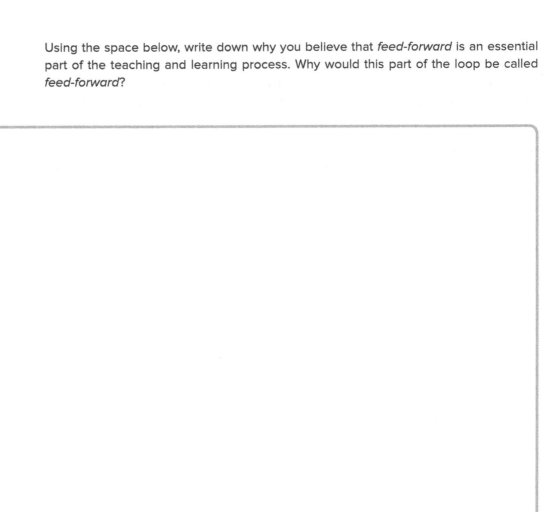

Feed-forward uses the information obtained during the learning experience to feed the learning process as we move forward in our schools and classrooms. Knowing where learners may need additional support, or where we may need to take a different approach to our teaching, clarifies where we are going next in the learning process. On the flip side, knowing where learners have met the learning intention and success criteria helps us and our learners know when we can move forward in the learning progression.

Feed-Forward Answers the Question *Where to next?*

Returning one last time to the metaphor of the musician and audience members, *feed-forward* would be the soundboard operator making note of the "in-the-moment" changes and including those in the set-up for the next concert. Musicians would use the information generated from feed-back to change their position on the stage or the way they played their instruments in future performances. For the audience members, this might involve them selecting different seats or locations throughout the concert venue.

How do you and your colleagues already engage in *feed-forward*? List specific strategies, practices, or examples in the space provided. We will come back to this later on in our work through the playbook.

Before closing out this module, we mentioned at the end of Module 2 (see page 21) that the T–P–E (adapted from Ritchhart et al., 2011) not only supports our learning in this playbook but also plays a role in effective feedback. Now that we have unpacked the three aspects of feedback—giving, receiving, and adjusting—and described how these three aspects interact through a continuous and dynamic feedback loop, how do you think the T–P–E strategy plays a role in effective feedback? Use the below space to jot down your ideas.

Take a moment to reflect on your learning. How are you progressing? Where do you need to spend a little more time in this module?

Consider these questions to guide your self-reflection and self-assessment:

1. Can I explain the three aspects of feedback?

2. Can I describe what is meant by "feedback as a continuous loop"?

3. Can I list the three questions most commonly associated with how feedback works?

Access videos and other resources at
resources.corwin.com/howfeedbackworks.

4

WHAT ARE THE FOUR FOUNDATIONAL ELEMENTS OF FEEDBACK?

LEARNING INTENTION

Next, we are learning about the four foundational elements that are necessary for feedback to work.

SUCCESS CRITERIA

We have successfully completed this module when

1. We can identify the four foundational elements.

2. We can analyze our own schools and classrooms across these four foundational elements.

3. We can explain why each of these foundational elements is essential and necessary for feedback to work.

4. We can relate these foundational elements to our prior learning about feedback (i.e., the previous modules).

As we move into our next module, let's review where we have been thus far in our learning journey. The following tasks are designed to generate evidence of your learning and create opportunities for feedback. However, we want you to try something with these tasks. Do the best you can to retrieve the prior learning without flipping back through the previous modules. Then, go back and verify your responses after working through the three tasks. This approach will become relevant in the upcoming modules.

As with the T–P–E strategy, these tasks not only support our learning but also set the stage for where we are going in this module.

Video 4.1: Introduction to Module 4

resources.corwin.com/ howfeedbackworks

Using the three-way Venn diagram below, compare and contrast *feed-up, feed-back,* and *feed-forward*.

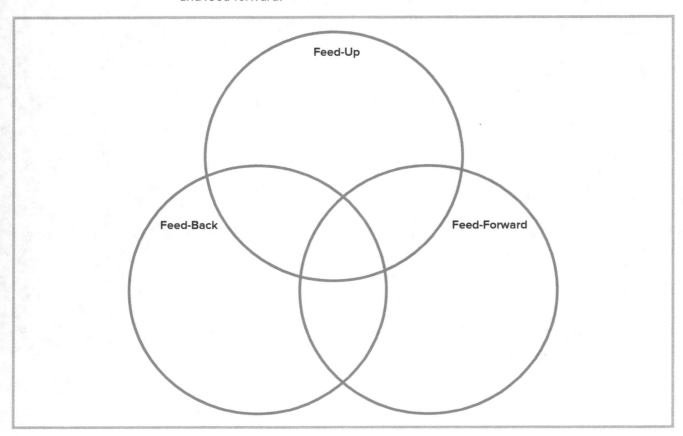

There are three aspects to *how feedback works.* What are those three aspects?

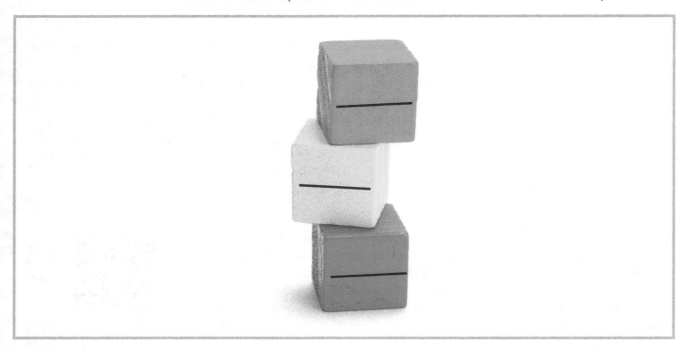

Image source: iStock.com/Michael Burrell

Finally, there are three questions that are addressed when *feedback works*. What are those three questions?

How did you do? What kind of feedback did you receive from simply looking back through previous modules? Were you able to generate information about where you were going, how you were going, and where you need to go next?

These three tasks reflect some, not all, of the foundation elements that allow feedback to work. In other words, to ensure that feed-up, feed-back, and feed-forward happen, these elements must be in place. To ensure the giving, receiving, and integrating of feedback happens each and every day, these elements must be in place. And finally, to set the stage for answering the three questions associated with feedback, these elements must be in place.

FOUNDATIONAL ELEMENTS THAT ALLOW FEEDBACK TO WORK

Before unpacking the foundational elements that allow feedback to work, use the Likert scale to pre-assess the presence of these foundational elements in your school or classroom. In addition to self-assessing with the Likert scale (always, sometimes, or never) provide specific examples that come to mind to support your self-scoring.

1. In my classroom, I generate visible evidence through instructional strategies and approaches.

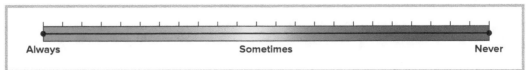

Always   Sometimes   Never

Examples to support my response:

2. Learners are engaged in their learning experiences and tasks while in my classroom.

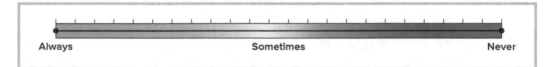

Always   Sometimes   Never

Examples to support my response:

3. My students and I hold the belief that challenge is a good thing in our classroom.

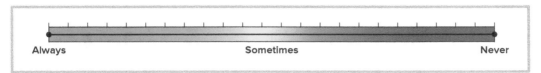

Always   Sometimes   Never

Examples to support my response:

4. Errors and mistakes are valued opportunities for learning in my classroom, and my students and I do not treat errors and mistakes as deficits or deficiencies in learning.

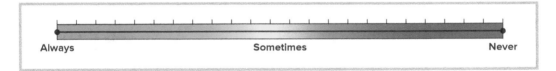

Always   Sometimes   Never

Examples to support my response:

5. All learners have equity of access and the opportunity to give and receive feedback during all learning experiences and tasks.

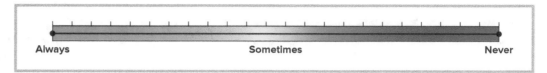

Always   Sometimes   Never

Examples to support my response:

6. Effective feedback focuses on the processes and products (i.e., the tasks), not the student—for example, "you are a good writer" versus "the word choice in your essay enhances the emotional response of the reader."

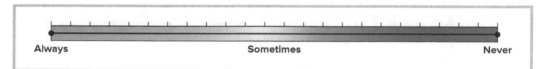

Always   Sometimes   Never

Examples to support my response:

7. Effective feedback and grades are not synonyms. (More on this later in the playbook.)

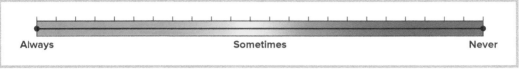

Always　　　　　　　　　　Sometimes　　　　　　　　　Never

Examples to support my response:

The foundational elements are beliefs and aspects of our classroom environments that foster, nurture, and sustain feedback that works. Without these elements, feedback fades away and the focus becomes grades, benchmarks, and punishments.

>>> Foundational Element 1

For feedback to work, there must be an atmosphere of mutual trust and respect in the classroom. Learners must feel safe in the learning environment to take on challenging tasks, be willing to make mistakes, and see mistakes as opportunities for growth. Teachers and learners must have established relationships that allow for the giving, receiving, and integrating of feedback. These relationships must start on the first day of the year, semester, or term and be nurtured during the entire year, semester, or term. If we do not have positive student-teacher and student-student relationships in our schools and classrooms, feedback will not work. We will see this in Modules 6 and 7.

> **For feedback to work, there must be an atmosphere of mutual trust and respect in the classroom.**

>>> Foundational Element 2

For feedback to work, teaching and learning must be visible in the classroom. What the learning is for the day, why that particular learning is important, and what successful learning looks like must be clear to both us and our learners. This is communicated through learning intentions, success criteria, and engaging tasks. We will devote a lot of time to this in Modules 8 through 10. This increases the strength of feedback by guiding both us and our learners about the specific focus of the feedback. Giving, receiving, and interpreting feedback about irrelevant or nonrelated content, skills, and understandings will diminish the value of the feedback.

 ## Foundational Element 3

For feedback to work, there must be evidence to gather and analyze during the learning process. Notice the word choice here: *evidence during the learning process* (Modules 10 and 15). This is more than just an exit ticket, quiz, or product. The learning experience must continuously make student thinking and learning visible to both us and our learners. To be quite frank about this particular element, for feedback to work, there must be something to give feedback on. The generation of evidence comes from the instructional strategies and approaches we use in our schools and classrooms.

 ## Foundational Element 4

For feedback to work, learners must be authentically engaged in a rigorous and relevant task. When a task does not generate authentic engagement, the type of engagement where learners take ownership of the learning, they are less likely to put forth effort into the learning process. Therefore, neither we nor our learners will know how they are *truly* progressing toward the learning outcomes and where we need to go next in our teaching. For example, if learners are not engaging in critical dialogue, asking genuine questions, engaging in self-reflection, or revising and editing their work, visible aspects of the learning process will not be valid or reliable. Communicating feedback is the focus of Modules 11 through 16.

Before we move forward in unpacking each of these foundational elements, return to your responses to the pre-assessment starting on page 40. In the margin, write down which foundational elements are intertwined in each of the statements. There may be multiple elements present in each statement. Once you finish this task, we are going to take on one more task before wrapping up this module.

FOUNDATIONAL ELEMENTS LEAD TO PRACTICES THAT ALLOW FEEDBACK TO WORK

Foundational elements, by themselves, do not make feedback work. Instead, they are our beliefs and aspects of our classroom environments that support the giving, receiving, and integrating of feedback. What actions or practices are already present in your classroom that reflect each of the foundational elements of feedback? Use the following chart to jot down your thinking. If you cannot think of any specific actions or practices, leave that space blank and use the third column to jot down ideas you might try. We provided a few examples to get you started.

Foundational Element	Current Actions or Practices	Ideas I Have
Foundational Element 1: For feedback to work, there must be an atmosphere of mutual trust and respect in the classroom.		
Foundational Element 2: For feedback to work, teaching and learning must be visible in the classroom.		**Example:** I need to be more consistent in sharing the daily learning intention.
Foundational Element 3: For feedback to work, there must be evidence to gather and analyze during the learning process.	**Example:** I have students write a summary of their learning in their interactive notebooks.	
Foundational Element 4: For feedback to work, learners must be authentically engaged in a rigorous and relevant task.		

Before closing out this module, we want to connect the dots of these first few modules. Flip back to Module 2, specifically page 19.

Do you remember that chart? You were asked to dive into the Meta^X database and explore the multi-dimensional aspects of feedback—aspects that are newer to the body of research on feedback. Some of those aspects are actually practices for giving, receiving, and integrating feedback. In the space below, list those influences that are specific feedback practices. We got the list started for you.

Practices:
1. Feedback with technology

2.

3.

4.

5.

6.

Using that list, add them to your chart above, matching them with the specific foundational element they support. Keep in mind that a single practice might be matched with multiple foundational elements. For example, *feedback with technology* has the potential to help with Foundational Element 1 because you can review a piece of writing through a learner's shared online document, listing the specific learning intention and criteria, providing a specific example, or simply placing a specific comment at the exact location in their writing that needs revising. This practice makes your teaching and their learning visible. But technology can also provide us the opportunity to observe a learner editing their piece of writing in real time and gain a better understanding of their thought process. Finally, providing feedback through a web-based document like Google Docs may be more comfortable for a learner than handing a rough draft back to them in class in front of their neighbors or peers.

Take a moment to match the practices above with the four foundational elements.

THE FOUR CS OF HOW FEEDBACK WORKS

We have devoted a lot of time to laying the foundation for how feedback works. From research to reality, we have developed a definition of feedback and the elements necessary for that feedback to be given, received, and integrated into the next steps in the learning process. Rather than try to memorize the foundational elements, we think about the Four Cs of how feedback works. Those Four Cs are

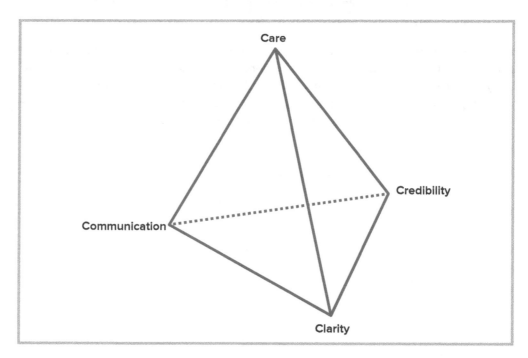

Flip back to page 3 in the introduction of this playbook. The following graphic should look very similar. However, instead of modules listed below each of the foundational elements, there is now blank space. In that blank space, please write in the **Four Cs of How Feedback Works**.

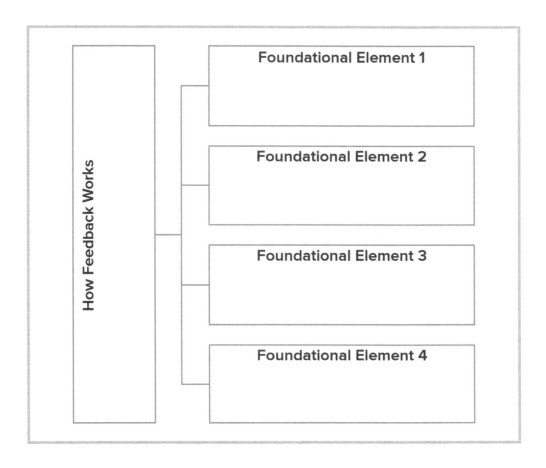

What happens when one or more of these elements is missing from our schools or classrooms? That is the focus of our next module: barriers to giving, receiving, and integrating feedback. Before turning to Module 5, rank the Four Cs in order of importance. Do you think one of the Cs is more critical than the others? Maybe you think they are all equitable in their contribution to effective feedback. Either way, write your thoughts in the space below.

Care and credibility set the foundation for who is giving, receiving, and integrating the feedback. Quality professional relationships allow both the give and receive to see each other with mutual trust and respect. When that relationship aligns with the credibility of who is giving, receiving, and integrating the feedback, the feedback loop has the potential to work at the highest level of efficiency and effectiveness. We will then turn our attention to the substance of the feedback. The C we are unpacking in those modules is clarity. Clarity sets the foundation for what is given, received, and integrated into where we are going next in our teaching and learning. We will close out the playbook by focusing on how to communicate feedback. The fourth and final C is communication.

So, away we go!

Take a moment to reflect on your learning. How are you progressing? Where do you need to spend a little more time in this module?

Consider these questions to guide your self-reflection and self-assessment:

1. Can I identify the four foundational elements?

2. Can I analyze our own schools and classrooms across these four foundational elements?

3. Can I explain why each of these foundational elements is essential and necessary for feedback to work?

4. Can I relate these foundational elements to our prior learning about feedback (i.e., the previous modules)?

online resources

Access videos and other resources at
resources.corwin.com/howfeedbackworks.

5

WHAT ARE THE BARRIERS TO GIVING, RECEIVING, AND INTEGRATING FEEDBACK?

LEARNING INTENTION

For this module, we are learning about the barriers that impede the exchange of feedback in our schools and classrooms.

SUCCESS CRITERIA

We have successfully completed this module when

1. We can describe the three triggers that impeded the feedback loop.

2. We can develop ways to recognize and respond to each of the three triggers.

3. We can explain how each of the triggers disrupts the feedback loop.

Video 5.1: Introduction to Module 5

resources.corwin.com/howfeedbackworks

Quick review: in the first column on the left, write in the Four Cs of how feedback works so that each of the Cs gets a separate row. Ignore the second column for now.

The Four Cs	What happens if it is missing?
_____	Giving: Receiving: Integrating:
_____	Giving: Receiving: Integrating:
_____	Giving: Receiving: Integrating:
_____	Giving: Receiving: Integrating:

Now we will turn our attention to the second column. In the space provided, write down how each aspect of feedback (i.e., giving, receiving, and integrating) is impeded when each of the Four Cs is absent from our school or classrooms.

As you completed the above chart, your mind likely generated specific examples from your own classroom where you tried to provide feedback to your learners and that feedback was not only ignored but also had no chance of being integrated into the learners' next steps of the learning process. If you completed this chart with colleagues, there was likely a lively, even if somewhat discouraging, conversation about learners not receiving or integrating feedback. Without causing too much stress and anxiety, can you think of a time when you were provided feedback and, for whatever reason, decided to tune out the giver of that feedback and had no intention of integrating their perspective into your future work?

Whether with our learners or our colleagues, there are situations where the giving, receiving, and integrating of feedback is blocked, bringing the feedback loop to a screeching halt. There is no feed-up, feed-back, or feed-forward—just fed-up learners and colleagues. For a playbook on how feedback works to, well, work, we must address this all-too-common situation.

What causes this situation? Use the space below to list the reasons you, your learners, and your colleagues block feedback. Be specific.

> Why do you, your learners, and your colleagues refuse to give, receive, or integrate feedback?

While starting the list above was tough, you likely had no problems filling in the box with reasons that you either have directly experienced or could easily imagine happening in your school or classroom. Believe it or not, there are researchers who have devoted a significant part of their career to uncovering why feedback often isn't registered.

Stone and Heen (2014) have devoted many years working in the public and private sectors seeking to understand what gets in the way of giving, receiving, and integrating feedback. What jams up the feedback loop from feeding-up, feeding-back, and feeding-forward to growth? The answer to this question is quite amazing and moves us forward in understanding how feedback works. But rather than tell you the answer, let's see if we can uncover it for ourselves by unpacking the following scenarios.

 **Example 1**

Martinez devoted a significant amount of time to developing her response to the writing prompt in her world history class. She was asked to take a position on what was meant by an "empire falling" and to support her claim with evidence. She engaged in research on the Roman Empire, the Chinese Empire, the Ottoman Empire, and the British Empire. She organized her thinking using a concept map and then developed a rough draft, asked her aunt to proofread her draft, and then prepared a final draft. She did not wait until the last minute to complete this assignment.

The feedback she's provided by her teacher, Mr. McClure, is very detailed and points to specific components in the rubric where she could improve her writing. However, all detailed feedback came after the teacher wrote on her paper, "You should not have waited until the last minute to write this essay. I believe if you had started sooner, you would not have had to rush to get something to turn in."

Using the space provided, write down your thoughts and reactions to this feedback. How do you think Martinez responded to this feedback?

We will return to each of these scenarios in just a moment. For now, we are just generating our thoughts and reactions to the scenarios.

>>> Example 2

Shawn and his classmates are trying to determine how to fence off a space for the class garden that maximizes the area of that space with the available resources provided to him and his classmates by the principal. Rather than do it for them, Ms. Snyder decided to let her students figure out how to best utilize the limited resources provided for this class project. In Ms. Snyder's seventh-grade science classroom, learners are used to tackling problems by developing possible solutions, giving each other feedback on those possible solutions, and then deciding which approach is the best one for that particular problem.

The principal, curious to see what Ms. Snyder and her students were going to do with the fencing and other supplies for the classroom, stops by to observe their progress. Ms. Markum does not usually just drop in for a visit; as soon as the principal walks through the door, Ms. Snyder's students notice and begin to speculate about the reasons for her visit. Ms. Markum calmly walks over and observes Shawn and his group looking at possible solutions. Ms. Markum warmly offers a suggestion and points out a mistake in the calculations on the chart paper. She smiles and exits the room.

Using the space provided, write down your thoughts and reactions to this feedback. How do you think Shawn and his classmates responded to this feedback?

 **Example 3**

Tula wants to be an artist. Tula talks about being an artist and relates everything she learned to art. When you talk to her, she will tell you, "This is who I am." She works very hard at developing her skills across multiple media. She practices all the elements of art (e.g., color, form, line, shape, space, texture, and value). For a fourth grader, she has developed many skills in the visual arts. Even though she only has art class once a week, she uses any spare time she has to create her own personal works of art. Last week, she began creating the illusion of depth on a two-dimensional surface. She chose to draw a particular area of the art room, varying the size of objects and overlapping certain objects to show that some objects appeared closer than others.

When she finished her sketch, she took her newly created piece of art to her art teacher. She wanted to get some feedback on her very first attempt at creating this illusion. Ms. Morris looks at the sketch and points out several positive aspects of Tula's work. Then Ms. Morris shares notes on some areas that need revising: "Tula, this object seems to be in the front and back of the sketch." Ms. Morris shows an example of another sketch to model how to adjust the size and overlap objects.

Using the space provided, write down your thoughts and reactions to this feedback. How do you think Tula responded to this feedback?

FEEDBACK BLOCKERS

Each one of the three scenarios involved a situation where the individuals, Martinez, Shawn, and Tula, either blocked the receiving and integrating of feedback or, at the very least, were hesitant in receiving and integrating. Furthermore, in each of the three instances, they are likely not to give feedback that would help Mr. McClure, Ms. Markum, or Ms. Morris receive feedback on their particular approach. In other words, the feedback loop was blocked.

Now let's return to the research of Stone and Heen (2014). In their extensive research spanning more than 15 years, they uncovered three major findings that are extremely relevant to our understanding of how feedback works. To make sense of this research, we are going to ask you to bring together your responses on page 50 regarding the absence of the Four Cs, your response on page 51 regarding why feedback is not received and integrated, and your thoughts on the three scenarios with Martinez, Shawn, and Tula on pages 52–54. Here are the three most relevant findings:

1. **Feedback given is not necessarily feedback received.** And while we may give feedback in our schools and classrooms, feedback only works when the other two aspects are present: receiving and integrating.

2. **There are certain triggers that cause our students, and us, to disregard feedback.** These triggers are a natural part of being human. Recognizing potential triggers and adjusting the feedback delivered can increase the potential that the feedback is received and integrated through the feedback loop.

3. **The giver of the feedback must look for and receive feedback about how they delivered the feedback.** Yeah, that is a tough sentence to process. Let's use our three scenarios as examples. As Mr. McClure, Ms. Markum, and Ms. Morris provide feedback, the feedback loop requires that they notice the responses of Martinez, Shawn, and Tula and receive that as feedback about their approach to the situations. This continuous adjusting, just like the musicians, soundboard operators, and audience members did in Module 3, depends on recognizing and responding to the triggers that may block feedback.

Types of Feedback Blockers

Stone and Heen (2014) identified three triggers that block feedback: identity triggers, truth triggers, and relationship triggers.

Identity Trigger

This particular type of trigger blocks our willingness to give, receive, and integrate feedback because it calls into question some aspect of our identity. When the feedback, regardless of who is offering that feedback, challenges our perception of our own strengths and weaknesses or how we think about ourselves, we turn our attention to saving face and not to receiving and integrating the feedback. In our classrooms, when learners that feel that their identity as a learner or person is called into question by the feedback, the feedback loop is blocked. Identity triggers are not about the substance of the feedback or the person delivering the feedback. Identity triggers are all about the receiver's perception of themselves.

Which one of the three scenarios is an example of an identity trigger? How does this trigger block the feedback loop in the specific scenario? How would you have adjusted your feedback to avoid an identity trigger?

Truth Trigger

If the feedback given to us is perceived as untrue, we will tune it out. A truth trigger can occur because our belief about the process or product is different from the person giving the feedback or as a result of the giver of the feedback not knowing about some aspect of the process or product. In our classrooms, we can block the feedback loop when the substance of our feedback does not match the reality of the learner. Truth triggers are all about the substance of the feedback and have nothing to do with the person delivering the feedback.

Which one of the three scenarios is an example of a truth trigger? How does this trigger block the feedback loop in the specific scenario? How would you have adjusted your feedback to avoid a truth trigger?

Relationship Trigger

A relationship trigger blocks the feedback loop when the receiver of the feedback does not believe the giver of the feedback should be the one, well, giving the feedback. In this particular situation, the blockage comes from who is delivering the feedback and not the substance of that feedback. If our response includes the question "who are they to give me feedback on my work?" we will probably not receive or integrate the information into where we go next. Relationship triggers have to do with who is giving the feedback.

Which one of the three scenarios is an example of a relationship trigger? How does this trigger block the feedback loop in the specific scenario? How would you have adjusted your feedback to avoid a relationship trigger?

Whew, we have really unpacked the idea of feedback blockers, those things that block the feedback loop. Now let's do something with this new learning.

If you remember, on page 55 we said that to understand feedback blockers we would ask you to bring together your responses on page 50 regarding the absence of the Four Cs, your response on page 51 regarding why feedback is not received and integrated, and your thoughts on the three scenarios with Martinez, Shawn, and Tula. We have tackled the last part of this work. You have now matched the three types of feedback blockers to the three scenarios. Let's now tie this in with the Four Cs and your own experiences.

In the following chart, use the second and third columns to process your learning about feedback blockers. First, summarize, in your own words, the three types of feedback blockers. Then note which of the Four Cs is missing in each of the feedback blockers. In other words, if you cause a truth trigger, which of the Four Cs might have led to that happening in your school or classroom? Oh, and the answer may include multiple Cs.

Feedback Blocker	Summarize this feedback blocker in your own words. Provide some examples.	Which of the Four Cs is missing and why do you think so?
Identity Trigger		
Truth Trigger		
Relationship Trigger		

Finally, return to your response on page 51 regarding why feedback is not received and integrated in your school or classroom. You likely can look through this list and recognize the existence of feedback blockers or triggers. As we close out this module, take a moment to pick three of those examples, identify those blockers or triggers, and describe what you can do in the future to avoid them.

Your Responses From Page 51	Which trigger is blocking the feedback in this situation?	What ideas or strategies do you have for avoiding this in the future?

For the remainder of this playbook, we will turn to the Four Cs, the foundational elements of how feedback works, our awareness of feedback blockers, and translate these ideas into classroom practices. These practices offer us the greatest potential for moving learning forward with feedback.

Take a moment to reflect on your learning. How are you progressing? Where do you need to spend a little more time in this module?

Consider these questions to guide your self-reflection and self-assessment:

1. Can I describe the three triggers that impeded the feedback loop?

2. Can I develop ways to recognize and respond to each of the three triggers?

3. Can I explain how each of the triggers disrupts the feedback loop?

 Access videos and other resources at
resources.corwin.com/howfeedbackworks.

PART II

THE FOUR Cs: CARE, CREDIBILITY, CLARITY, AND COMMUNICATION

In this section:

WHAT IS THE ROLE OF *CARE* IN HOW FEEDBACK WORKS?

LEARNING INTENTION

As we begin to look at each of the Four Cs, in this module we are learning about the role of care in supporting the feedback loop in our schools and classrooms.

SUCCESS CRITERIA

We have successfully completed this module when

1. We can describe what is meant by care.

2. We can identify the characteristics of positive and productive relationships in our schools and classrooms.

3. We can identify specific strategies that foster, nurture, and sustain positive and productive relationships.

4. We can explain how care supports the feedback loop.

Video 6.1: Introduction to Module 6

resources.corwin.com/ howfeedbackworks

Feedback works when there are there is an atmosphere of mutual trust and respect in the classroom. Flip back to page 58 in the previous module. Where did you place the **care** in the chart? When **care** is missing from our schools and classrooms, there is an increased possibility of an identity trigger, a truth trigger, and, most certainly, a relationship trigger. But what do you mean by care? Care incorporates the teacher-teacher, teacher-student, and student-student relationships in our schools and classrooms that create an atmosphere of mutual trust and respect. As we said before, learners must feel safe in the learning environment to take on challenging tasks, be willing to make mistakes, and see mistakes as opportunities for growth. These established relationships allow for the giving, receiving, and integrating of feedback. These relationships allow us to be more aware of our feedback to and from each other so that we can recognize and respond to the three triggers that block the feedback loop.

If you were to ask the three of us what matters most in teaching and learning overall, not just feedback, we would tell you that it is our positive and productive relationships in our classrooms. These relationships are the foundation of everything we do in our classrooms. The same is likely true for you.

SUPPORTING CARE THROUGH TEACHER–TEACHER RELATIONSHIPS

To unpack the role of teacher-teacher relationships, take a look at several reflective questions. To avoid any awkwardness in your work through this playbook, we do not expect you to write down your responses to these questions. After all, this is a module about relationships, and we do not want your responses to tarnish relationships in the process.

> Who are the individuals from whom you are *always willing* to take feedback?
>
> Who are some individuals from whom you are *reluctant* to take feedback?
>
> Now, think about how the individuals on these two lists are different.

Our guess is that the most striking difference between the two lists is that you have a very different relationship with those from whom you are always willing to take feedback than the second list. Likewise, the quality of the relationship between us and our colleagues is foundational to the giving, receiving, and integrating of feedback about our own teaching. The teacher-teacher relationships in our schools are fueled by

1. Mutual respect

2. Trust

3. Embracing diverse perspectives

4. Empathy

5. Communication

When care is missing from our schools and classrooms, there is an increased possibility of identity, truth, and relationship triggers.

Together, these five characteristics of quality professional relationships allow for critical conversations about all aspects of learning (e.g., cognitive, emotional, social, behavioral, and dispositional). With regard to feedback, teacher-teacher relationships support the effective and efficient workings of the feedback loop about our own schools.

Let's revisit the characteristics of quality professional relationships. Fill those into the first column of the following chart.

Characteristics of Quality Professional Relationships (Teacher-Teacher)	How would I know if these characteristics are present in my school? In other words, what are the look-fors that give you confidence these are present in your school?	What strategies or approaches could we take to improve on this specific characteristic?
1.		
2.		
3.		
4.		
5.		

SUPPORTING CARE THROUGH TEACHER–STUDENT RELATIONSHIPS

Now let's turn our attention to teacher-student relationships. Rita Pierson pointed out in her popular TED Talk that students don't learn from teachers they don't like.

This idea, well supported by research (see Cornelius-White, 2007; Hattie, 2009; Visible Learning Meta[X], 2022), implies that students don't receive and integrate feedback from teachers they don't like either. Yes, our learners have a greater potential to move forward in their learning when there are positive teacher-student relationships. Just as there are essential characteristics of teacher-teacher relationships, there are those characteristics that foster, nurture, and sustain quality relationships between us and our learners (Cornelius-White, 2007, p. 113):

1. Teacher empathy

2. Unconditional positive regard

3. Genuineness

4. Non-directivity

5. Encouragement of critical thinking

Video 6.2: Rita Pierson's TED Talk

resources.corwin.com/ howfeedbackworks

Source: https://youtu.be/ SFnMTHhKdkw

Just as we did with the characteristics of teacher-teacher relationships, let's take a moment to process these five characteristics. Using any resources you have available to you (phone, computer, books, etc.), come up with your own summarized description or definition of each of these features. We have provided a reflective question to help you frame your summary. Then, use the third column in the chart to list strategies or approaches you use or would consider using to support each characteristic.

Characteristics of Positive Student-Teacher Characteristics	Summarize what this means in your own words.	What strategies or approaches could we take to improve on this specific characteristic?
Teacher Empathy *Reflective Question:* **How do you and your students seek connections with each other?**		

(Continued)

(Continued)

Characteristics of Positive Student-Teacher Characteristics	Summarize what this means in your own words.	What strategies or approaches could we take to improve on this specific characteristic?
Unconditional Positive Regard *Reflective Question:* How will you and your students know you care about each other as people?		
Genuineness *Reflective Question:* How will you and your students know you care about each other as learners?		
Non-Directivity *Reflective Question:* How will you and your students know you hold each other's abilities in high regard?		
Encouragement of Critical Thinking *Reflective Question:* How will you and your students know that you both value each other's thinking over facts?		

Before we move forward in this module, take some time to jot down the Four Cs. Flip back to previous modules for a quick hint.

1.

2.

3.

4.

While we address the Four Cs in separate parts of this playbook, we want to be clear that these four foundational elements interact with each other to support the giving, receiving, and integrating of feedback through the feedback loop. For example, strong teacher-teacher and teacher-student relationships rely on effective communication. This effective communication includes teachers feeling comfortable giving feedback to their colleagues and students feeling comfortable giving feedback to their teachers.

Quality teacher-teacher and teacher-student relationships require clarity around what the expectations are in the learning environment, the relevance of those expectations, and a clear understanding of what success looks like in the learning experience. We will devote the entirety of Module 8 of the playbook to clarity. Finally, there must be established credibility between the giver, receiver, and substance of the feedback. This will be addressed in Module 7.

> The four foundational elements interact with each other to support the giving, receiving, and integrating of feedback through the feedback loop.

SUPPORTING CARE THROUGH STUDENT–STUDENT RELATIONSHIPS

Student-student relationships matter both in general and with regard to feedback. Flip back to Module 2, pages 19–20. We want to look at two of the influences related to feedback: peer feedback and self-feedback.

What is the effect size for **peer feedback** (peer assessment and grading)? _____

What is the effect size for **self-feedback**? _____

You likely recalled the striking difference between the potential influence of peer-to-peer feedback and self-feedback. This would suggest that engaging our learners in giving, receiving, and integrating feedback from their classmates is important in their learning progress. However, this then requires us to teach them how to engage in the feedback loop with their shoulder partner, seat neighbor, or group member.

In the space below, list the characteristics of quality teacher-teacher relationships and teacher-student relationships. You should have a total of 10 characteristics.

Characteristics

1.

2.

3.

4.

5.

6.

7.

8.

9.

10.

The goal of this particular task is to develop a list of characteristics you would look for in your own school or classroom that are necessary to support student-student relationships. Just repeating all 10 characteristics is unreasonable in a single classroom and quite likely redundant. So, with your colleagues or on your own, decide which of those characteristics you would like to develop in your own learners. List those in the first column of the below chart.

Characteristics	How will you and your colleagues build the capacity in your learners for each of these characteristics? Be specific.

Then, in the column on the right, describe how you will build the capacity in your learners around those agreed-upon characteristics.

The characteristics you identified and the plan for building those characteristics into your school or classroom are vital in laying a foundation of **care**. Plus, it helps us to be more intentional in our interactions with learners when we know we are supporting our learners in navigating the feedback loop.

Before we complete this module, we want to spend a bit of time discussing the relationship between all three of these relationships: teacher-teacher, teacher-student, and student-student. Quite simply put, how we relate to our colleagues and our students strongly influences how they relate to each other. Let's consider two examples.

Example 1

Miranda is a student in Ms. Campbell's second-grade classroom. During small group time, the learners are flexibly grouped and move through a series of thematic learning stations that integrate the major concepts articulated in the day's learning intentions. Each station has a set of success criteria and a means for students to make their thinking and learning visible.

Miranda arrives at the center that focused on generating and analyzing patterns. While she can read the directions and success criteria, she is a bit unclear on how she was to make her thinking and learning visible. She is overheard telling one of her classmates, "I just don't know what I am supposed to do here." Miranda decides to raise her hand and ask Ms. Campbell. Ms. Campbell, after releasing a big sigh, says, "Miranda, you should have listened better to the directions. I can't help you right now."

What is your initial reaction to this example? How might this exchange between Miranda and Ms. Campbell influence teacher-student relationships in the classroom? What about student-student relationships?

>>> **Example 2**

Later that day, Miranda is in Ms. Wingfield's music classroom. As you might suspect, this is a very active and loud classroom. However, Ms. Wingfield has several cues and rein-forcements (more on that later) to support the learning in her classroom. Ms. Wingfield tells her students, "Musicians, please find page 12 in your sheet music and place your mallets on Middle C." Miranda is not completely clear on which piece of music they would be playing on the xylophones, nor is she completely sure about the location of Middle C. Ms. Wingfield is walking around the room watching her learners navigate this set of instructions and notices (more on that later as well) that Miranda hesitated. After a slight pause, Ms. Wingfield quickly adds this to her instructions: "Musicians, check in with your neighbor and see if they have located the correct sheet music and located Middle C. If they haven't, give them some assistance. When you are both ready, give me a thumbs up."

What is your initial reaction to this example? How might this exchange between Miranda and Ms. Campbell influence teacher-student relationships in the classroom? What about student-student relationships?

Our students know how we are feeling at most points in the day. Because our learn-ers spend all day with us for an entire academic year, they get good at reading the social environment of the classroom. They notice and file away how we interact with our colleagues and with other students. This noticing and filing away serve as a model for how they should interact in the school and classroom, whether positive or negative. We must make sure we do not create a chilly climate in our schools and classrooms.

A "CHILLY" CLASSROOM

In 1987, Good conducted a study of the differential teacher treatment of students and found that low-achieving students

1.   Are criticized more often for failure.

2.   Are praised less than their peers.

3.   Receive less feedback.

4.   Are called on less often.

5.   Have less eye contact with the teacher.

6.   Have fewer friendly interactions with the teacher.

7.   Experience acceptance of their ideas less often.

In a chilly classroom climate, students do not feel they are valued and instead feel that "their presence . . . is at best peripheral, and at worst an unwelcome intrusion" (Hall & Sandler, 1982, p. 3). Now, before we cause an identity, truth, or relationship trigger, let's unpack this just a bit more.

Use the space below to explain how sharing the chilly classroom research with a colleague might cause all three feedback blockers.

Sharing this research with you is not meant to be accusatory or critical of your own learning environment. Many of the behaviors in the chilly climate are likely not intentional or deliberate. As teachers, we tend to connect with students who connect with us. Instead, we want to close out this module with an awareness of these behaviors in hopes of consciously trying to build relationships with all our learners. This is part of how feedback works and how learning works.

Below are several reflective questions that can help us think about the climate in our classroom and the building of quality professional relationships in our schools and classrooms.

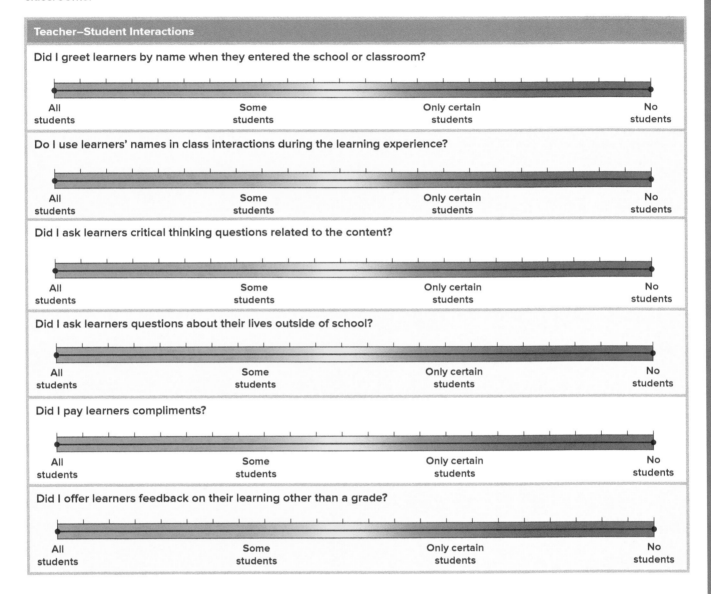

Teacher–Student Interactions

Did I greet learners by name when they entered the school or classroom?

All students — Some students — Only certain students — No students

Do I use learners' names in class interactions during the learning experience?

All students — Some students — Only certain students — No students

Did I ask learners critical thinking questions related to the content?

All students — Some students — Only certain students — No students

Did I ask learners questions about their lives outside of school?

All students — Some students — Only certain students — No students

Did I pay learners compliments?

All students — Some students — Only certain students — No students

Did I offer learners feedback on their learning other than a grade?

All students — Some students — Only certain students — No students

Every interaction we have with our colleagues and learners is an opportunity to have an impact. That impact may come in the form of learning across all domains (e.g., cognitive, emotional, social, behavioral, and dispositional). That impact may come in the form of feedback—the very focus of our work together. Without quality professional relationships, the potential for our impact is greatly diminished. But what happens if we do not have the same opportunity to interact with certain colleagues and certain learners? Please do not take offense to this next statement, but we believe that it is our fault—not our colleagues' and certainly not our students'. Creating those interactions is up to us as individuals. As we close out this module, consider the different ways you can create interactions that build relationships and offer opportunities for feedback.

How will you ensure all learners have the opportunity to share their thinking and learning?	
How will you notice who hasn't participated, or had an opportunity to share their thinking and learning so you can create that interaction?	
What will you need to be mindful of to create more opportunities for learners to interact with you and each other?	
How will you be a presence during student-student interactions?	
How will you connect with learners or create connections beyond the content, skills, and understandings in your school or classroom?	
How will you connect with families and community members that also know your learners?	

High levels of positive relationships build trust and make our classrooms a safe place to give, receive, and integrate feedback. In turn, this makes our school a safe place for learning—closing the gap between where we are and where we are going. Indeed, powerful teacher-teacher, teacher-student, and student-student relationships allow all of us to embrace opportunities for feedback. A lot of us avoid situations where we may receive feedback. This avoidance is likely due to our experience with the three feedback blockers. However, quality professional relationships lay the foundation for the givers of the feedback to recognize and avoid the three triggers and, at the same time, lay the foundation for us to receive and integrate the feedback into where we are going next. The same applies to our learners.

Care is only one of the Cs. Relationships alone are not enough. We now turn to the next C, **credibility**.

Take a moment to reflect on your learning. How are you progressing? Where do you need to spend a little more time in this module?

Consider these questions to guide your self-reflection and self-assessment:

1. Can I describe what is meant by care?

2. Can I identify the characteristics of positive and productive relationships in our schools and classrooms?

3. Can I identify specific strategies that foster, nurture, and sustain positive and productive relationships?

4. Can I explain how care supports the feedback loop?

Access videos and other resources at
resources.corwin.com/howfeedbackworks.

WHAT IS THE ROLE OF *CREDIBILITY* IN HOW FEEDBACK WORKS?

LEARNING INTENTION

Next, we focus our learning on the role of credibility in supporting the feedback loop in our schools and classrooms.

SUCCESS CRITERIA

We have successfully completed this module when

1. We can explain the four components of credibility.

2. We can connect credibility with the three triggers that disrupt the feedback loop.

3. We can identify specific strategies that foster, nurture, and sustain credibility for each member of our school and classroom community.

4. We can explain how credibility supports the feedback loop.

Video 7.1: Introduction to Module 7

resources.corwin.com/ howfeedbackworks

Before we unpack the second C, **credibility**, we have to first make sure we know what the term means. What does *credibility* mean? What does it mean for a person to be credible? Grab your phone, computer, or dictionary and summarize the meaning of *credibility*.

Summarize your understanding of credibility. In addition, explain what you believe it means for a teacher or the students to be credible.

Credibility, in general, is a quality attributed to an individual if they are to be trusted, believed in, or convincing in whatever position they are taking. Our hope is that your summary above spoke to these characteristics and extended to us and our students.

➡ Are we trusted by our colleagues and students?

➡ Do our colleagues and students believe us when we say something?

➡ When we speak about a specific topic or situation, are we convincing?

As you might have guessed, credibility is a foundational element of feedback. If we are not credible, feedback will not work. If our learners are not credible, feedback will not work. Credibility holds a place as one of the Cs because without credibility, we are not likely to engage in the feedback loop, blocking the receiving and integrating of any feedback we are given.

As a quick review, we've listed the three feedback blockers discussed in the earlier modules. Next to each feedback blocker, describe how high and low credibility influence the triggers.

Credibility, in general, is a quality attributed to an individual if they are to be trusted, believed in, or convincing.

Feedback Blockers	How does high credibility influence this trigger?	How does low credibility influence this trigger?
Identity trigger		
Truth trigger		
Relationship trigger		

CREDIBILITY MAKES FEEDBACK WORK

General credibility is one thing, teacher credibility is a bit different. On pages 76–77 of this module, you were asked to link credibility to teaching and learning in your school or classroom. While teacher credibility involves trust and belief, the research on credibility focuses more on a different question with regard to credibility. In the classroom, credibility comes down to this key question: Do your students believe they can learn from you?

If your students answer that question with a yes, you have credibility with your learners. In addition to seeing growth in their learning, you will also see an increased willingness to engage in the feedback loop. To be quite frank about it, if you have credibility with your learners, they are much more likely to give, receive, and integrate feedback with you. Furthermore, you will probably avoid inadvertently blocking feedback through one or more of the triggers. Given the importance of credibility in how feedback works, let's pick this idea apart a bit more. What is needed to create or enhance credibility?

THE COMPONENTS OF CREDIBILITY

In their 2009 meta-analysis, Finn et al. (2009) looked at multiple dimensions of credibility and found that teacher credibility has the potential to more than double the rate of learning in the classroom. No doubt, this accelerated hike in learning is due in part to the willingness to give, receive, and integrate feedback.

In addition to their exploration of these dimensions, they also point out that credibility is dynamic—always changing, depending on the context. Before we look at the components of credibility, we want to spend a little time on the idea of credibility being a dynamic C.

Why do you think credibility is a dynamic C? What factors cause the credibility of a teacher or student to change?

Look back at your answer to the above question. Did you include words or phrases that resemble trust, competence, passion, or relatability? Maybe you did not use those exact words but explained that credibility comes from being trustworthy or doing what you say you are going to do. Did you mention that teachers who are good at teaching, as perceived by the learners, are more credible? What about showing that we are passionate about particular content? You might have mentioned something about being able to relate to someone.

Using any resources you have available to you (e.g., phone, computer, books), come up with your own summarized description or definition of each of the dimensions of credibility. Then, use the second column in the chart to list strategies or approaches you use or would consider using to support each characteristic.

Dimensions of Credibility	What strategies or approaches could we take to improve on this specific dimension?
Do my students trust me?	
How do I show that I am competent as a teacher?	
Do I show passion for teaching and learning?	
How do I connect with my learners?	

These are the four dimensions of credibility and give us insight into how we monitor and assess our credibility, as well as our students' credibility. Let's take a deep dive into the four dimensions of credibility further and identify ways to foster, nurture, and sustain credibility for the sake of feedback.

TRUST

Whether providing feedback on a narrative essay, the solution to a mathematics problem, or the response to an open-ended question in social studies, if the learners do not trust that you have their best interest in mind, they are less likely to hear what you have to say about their learning. Likewise, if learners do not trust each other, peer-to-peer feedback will come to a standstill as well.

As an example, Rhondae is engaged in a station on overhand throwing in his physical education class. This week, second graders are learning the mechanics of overhand throwing and transferring that skill to hitting a target. While Ms. Berrang is moving around the gymnasium, she is offering feedback to learners about their cues and modifying their form to better hit the target. Rhondae knows he was going to get feedback because he could not remember the cues nor was he regularly hitting the target. However, Ms. Berrang walks by Rhondae and simply says, "Good job, Rhondae, keep it up."

What is your initial reaction to this example? How might this exchange between Rhondae and Ms. Berrang influence Ms. Berrang's credibility with Rhondae?

This quick moment likely cost Ms. Berrang credibility with Rhondae. This brief exchange likely called into question Rhondae's belief that Ms. Berrang cares about him as an individual in the physical education class and had his best learning interests in mind. Take a few moments and consider these suggestions for building and maintaining trust in your school or classroom. There is a slight twist with this task. The column on the left contains the suggestion. However, the right column asks you to identify actions that can be done if we inadvertently do something to jeopardize that trust.

Suggestion	Action
Do what we say we are going to do . . . at all times.	What happens if we say something to our learners but don't follow through?
Be specific, accurate, and concise with feedback to a learner.	What should we do if we are not truthful in our feedback to a learner (e.g., we are worried that it will upset them too much)?
Be proactive in our feedback instead of waiting for learners to make a mistake.	What happens if we only catch learners making a mistake?
Avoid stereotypes or other negative feelings about specific learners.	What happens if specific learners evoke negative feelings in us (e.g., they are learners that really know how to push our buttons)?

We know that the column on the right was difficult. However, let's be honest, we have all been there in our own schools and classrooms. We promised to do one thing, and we were unable to follow through. We have held back our feedback because a learner seems to be having a more difficult than usual day. What about that learner who we seem to only catch doing something wrong or seems to raise our anxiety and stress? This is not easy. However, we must ensure that trust is developed and maintained in our schools and classrooms. As we mentioned in the previous module, how we handle this serves as a model for our learners. One additional piece of research may be helpful here. Hoy and Tschannen-Moran (1999) identified five elements for trust to be developed and maintained:

➡ **Benevolence:** Confidence that our learner's well-being or something they care about will be protected by us as their teacher. This includes the confidence that we will not exploit their weaknesses or areas for growth.

➡ **Honesty:** We must accept responsibility for our actions as the teacher and not distort the truth in order to shift blame to someone else in our school or classroom.

➡ **Openness:** When appropriate, we must be transparent with our learners and let them see how and why things came about the way that they did.

➡ **Reliability:** We must be consistent with our behavior and know what to expect from our learners.

➡ **Competency:** We must grow personally and professionally to ensure we maintain our knowledge and skills as a teacher (adapted from Hoy & Tschannen-Moran, 1999).

Describe the ways you will develop and maintain trust using the five elements adapted from Hoy and Tschannen-Moran (1999).

COMPETENCE

Competence is a tough one. To illustrate this point, think back to an individual whose feedback you value above all others. Who is that individual? Is that person an expert in the field or area of the feedback? Do they have a parade of degrees in the area of the feedback? This is just a guess, but we wonder if that individual is exceptional at explaining things in a way that helps you make meaning of the feedback. Maybe that individual has been through experiences that lead you to trust that "they know what they are talking about." This is competence. Consider two examples to further highlight this point.

≫ Example 1

Salvador submits his essay to Ms. Coyner, his eighth-grade language arts teacher, on the role of weather in the decisions made by the axis and allied powers in World War II. As part of the feedback process, Ms. Coyner conferences with her learners and goes over the writing rubric with each learner. Salvador's turn is next. Ms. Coyner does not have a degree in history or world cultures. She recognizes that she does not know as much about this topic as Salvador does. Her approach during the conference involved asking Salvador questions about the flow of his essay and the level of detail supporting his argument. "Salvador, right here, I feel like something is missing. Are there additional details that would help someone like me learn more about your perspective? I think you should revise this and include some additional details about the particular weather and military campaign." She points out that she wants the reader "to get just as excited about this topic as you." Salvador immediately returns to his laptop and begins to flesh out those details. When asked about his writing conference, Salvador states, "Ms. Coyner's feedback is so helpful and really helps me improve my writing."

Why do you think Salvador was so willing to receive feedback from Ms. Coyner regarding his essay on a history topic? Be specific.

》》》 Example 2

The bell rings and Salvador transitions across the hallway to his Algebra I class. Dr. Allen is the mathematics teacher on this eighth-grade team and teaches all levels of mathematics. Prior to joining the middle school faculty, he worked at a university. His doctorate is in mathematics education and he holds master's and bachelor's degrees in pure mathematics. The situation in this classroom turns out a bit different than the one in Ms. Coyner's classroom. Salvador is quick to share that "when Dr. Allen tries to explain what I need to work on in mathematics, I don't understand what he is trying to tell me. He knows so much about mathematics, and I feel like I can't keep up. He isn't really good at giving feedback. Most of the time I just pretend to listen and then get my friends to help me at lunch or on the way home."

Why do you think Salvador was so resistant to receive feedback from Dr. Allen in Algebra I? Be specific.

Now let us be clear. Content knowledge is very important, and these two examples are not meant to diminish the value of strong background knowledge in any content area or discipline. The point we are trying to illustrate is that competence is not based solely on years of experience, degrees earned, or a particular job title. Salvador wants to know that his teachers both have the content, skills, and understandings related to a particular subject or discipline and can relate that information in a way that moves his learning forward. Salvador expects an appropriate level of expertise and accuracy from his teachers. However, his belief about the competence of his teachers is measured by the ability of the teacher to deliver content, skills, and understandings in a coherent and organized manner.

The willingness of us and our learners to enter into the feedback loop works the same way. While expertise is a part of the equation, the communication of that expertise is equally important. We have all been there—someone who is clearly competent in a particular skill, craft, or area but unable to share that knowledge in a way that helps others learn. Take a few moments and consider these suggestions for building and maintaining trust in your school or classroom. As earlier, there is a slight twist with this task; while the column on the left contains the suggestion, the column on the right asks you to identify actions that can be done if we inadvertently do something to jeopardize that trust.

Suggestion	Action
Before engaging in the feedback loop, we should make sure we know the content, skills, and understandings related to the feedback.	What happens if we do not have a background in a particular content, skill, or understanding?
Prepare or plan how you will deliver the feedback, ensuring the feedback is clear, coherent, and cohesive.	What should we do if we are not clear on how we should organize feedback?
Practice and monitor voice tone, facial expressions, and other forms of nonverbal communication.	What happens if we unintentionally communicate something different through nonverbal communication?

There is one more thing we would like you to consider before we look at the third dimension of credibility. How does **care** interact with **credibility**?

Describe the ways you will develop, monitor, and maintain credibility.

DYNAMISM

When we are receiving feedback from someone, their affective or dispositional characteristics have a significant impact on whether we take that feedback and integrate the information into where we go next. If the individual giving the feedback is positive, excited, and eager to see us move forward in our learning, that energy is contagious and motivates us to integrate the information into our next steps. Likewise, if we see learners engaged and motivated in a learning experience, we are often drawn to that

This dimension of credibility focuses on the passion we and our learners bring to the learning environment and experience.

excitement and are more likely to engage in critical dialogue around their learning. The exchange of feedback is easier and more natural when we are dynamic. This dimension of credibility focuses on the passion we and our learners bring to the learning environment and experience. This passion manifests itself as authentic engagement, where we take ownership of our teaching and learning.

However, we can let dynamism lead us to avoid those who do not seem to be as passionate about teaching and learning. If the feedback loop is helped along by being dynamic about the content, skills, and understandings in our schools and classrooms, what strategies would you use to nudge those individuals into giving, receiving, and integrating feedback?

In addition to the list you just generated, here are some suggestions for generating dynamism in your schools and classrooms:

1. **Be genuine and authentic in your excitement.** Overselling the excitement can throw up feedback blockers like the truth trigger or relationship trigger. If you are overly excited and the learner believes you are just trying to make them feel better, this will fall flat. The same goes for peer-to-peer feedback. This will diminish credibility.

2. **Break the feedback down into smaller steps or chunks so that the receiver of the feedback can experience success as soon as possible.** Success

leads to more success. If we and our learners flood each other with too much feedback, and we already lack dynamism, this will just exacerbate the problem.

3. **Make the learning experience relevant.** While this suggestion extends beyond the purpose of this playbook, we would be remiss if we did not mention the relevancy and authenticity of the learning experience. Learning, and consequently feedback, is hard to be passionate about if we struggle to find relevancy in the learning experience. If we and our learners simply do not care, we will be resistant to feedback.

4. **Collaborate.** This final suggestion draws from pages 3 and 4 in the introduction of this playbook. If you need a moment to flip back and review that section, go for it. Whoever you selected to work alongside in this playbook, get ideas and feedback from them on your dynamism. Remember, be dynamic in your request for feedback.

We provided four suggestions for generating dynamism. We likely left some things off the list. Please use the space below to add to the list. Describe the ways you will generate passion about teaching and funnel that passion to your learning environment.

IMMEDIACY

This concept, the fourth dimension of credibility, was first introduced in 1971. Psychologist Albert Mehrabian (1971) discovered the social phenomenon that we tend to lean into those individuals that we like and find relatable during social interactions. For example, you likely have students that stop by your classroom to just visit or "hang out." These learners make a conscious choice to spend their free time in your classroom. Have you ever asked yourself why? Furthermore, these learners likely ask for your advice (aka, feedback) on different aspects of their lives. This may be related to things beyond reading, writing, and arithmetic. Again, have you ever asked yourself why?

Just as the concept of immediacy or relatability promotes a quality positive relationship and credibility, this concept is key to the effective exchange of feedback. We are more likely to feed-up, feed-back, and feed-forward when we and our learners can relate to each other in our schools and classrooms. Immediacy, or relatability between our learners, comes from

1. **Sharing and respecting the values of each member of the school and classroom community.** Immediacy is supported when we acknowledge and respect how others see the world. In your classroom, how do you promote the diversity, equity, and inclusion of different perspectives, experiences, and approaches?

2. **Recognizing that each individual in your school or classroom has strengths and skills that positively contribute to the community.** In your learning environment, how do you recognize and elevate the assets of every member of the school or classroom community?

3. **Valuing each member of the community.** Each and every colleague and student is a valued member of the community and should be actively engaged in the school and classroom community. How do we design our school and classrooms so that each member of the community is actively contributing to our success?

4. **Being a bucket filler.** This is our favorite way to enhance immediacy or relatability. Every interaction is an opportunity to add value to someone's day. To foster immediacy, we must take these opportunities as often as possible. What do you do to add value to your colleagues and your learners?

This goes without saying, but upping our immediacy and relatability ups our capacity to give, receive, and integrate feedback.

Make a list of strategies that will enhance the immediacy and relatability of each member of your school and classroom community. We will provide some examples to get you started. Come on! We want to see if you can fill up the entire box with ideas.

- Look at students and smile while talking.
- Learn their names before the year starts and call students by name.
- Use *we* and *us* to refer to the class.

We cannot emphasize enough the importance of credibility in the flow of feedback between us and our learners. When an individual is perceived as not credible, the willingness to engage with that individual comes to a screeching halt. Learning is blocked and the giving, receiving, and integrating of feedback is stopped. We likely experience truth triggers, identity triggers, and certainly relationship triggers. The four dimensions of teacher credibility—trust, competence, dynamism, and immediacy—can help do just that. As a final task for this module, now that you have a sense of the value of credibility, complete the following self-check.

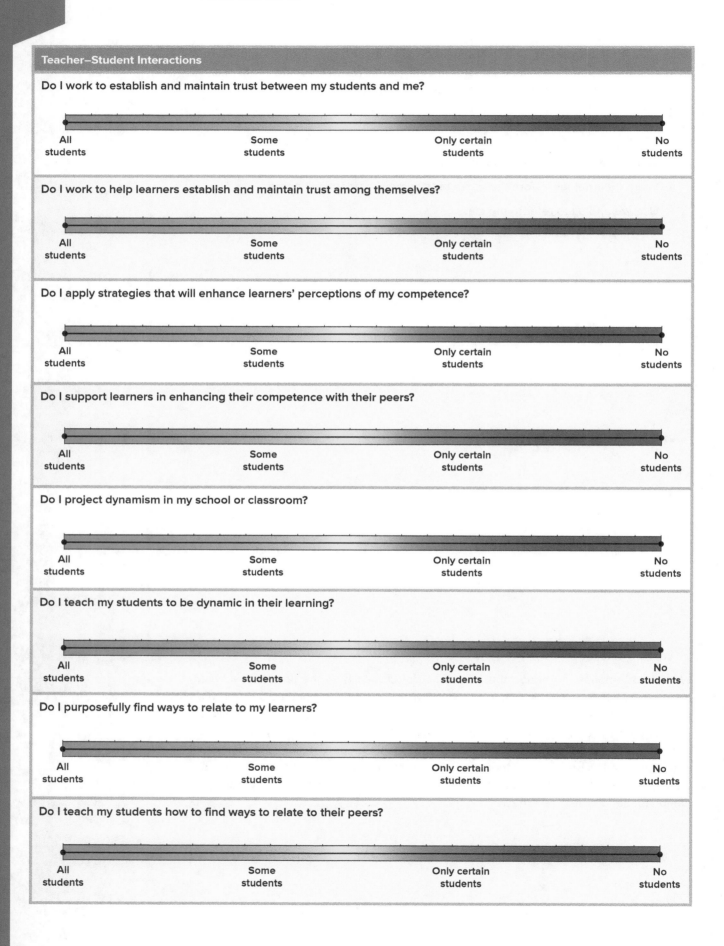

Teacher–Student Interactions

Do I work to establish and maintain trust between my students and me?

| All students | Some students | Only certain students | No students |

Do I work to help learners establish and maintain trust among themselves?

| All students | Some students | Only certain students | No students |

Do I apply strategies that will enhance learners' perceptions of my competence?

| All students | Some students | Only certain students | No students |

Do I support learners in enhancing their competence with their peers?

| All students | Some students | Only certain students | No students |

Do I project dynamism in my school or classroom?

| All students | Some students | Only certain students | No students |

Do I teach my students to be dynamic in their learning?

| All students | Some students | Only certain students | No students |

Do I purposefully find ways to relate to my learners?

| All students | Some students | Only certain students | No students |

Do I teach my students how to find ways to relate to their peers?

| All students | Some students | Only certain students | No students |

APPROACHING THE HALF-WAY POINT OF OUR WORK

As you prepare to move into the next C, we wanted to stop for a moment to reflect on where we have been so far. Over the past seven modules, we have rolled up our sleeves and unpacked how feedback works. Simply put, the answer to the question *how does feedback work?* is complex. We know that and are so glad you are with us on this journey. Flip back to page 20 in Module 2. The takeaways from your deep dive into the research on feedback are worth revisiting, especially the first two items on that list. We have provided them below with a few of the words missing. Return to page 20 and fill in those missing words.

1. Feedback is _____ and cannot be treated as a

   _____ concept.

2. There are now previously unstudied and _____ aspects to feedback

   (reinforcement and cues, self, technology, timing, etc.) and having a _____ view

   of feedback is not sufficient in advancing learning in our schools and classrooms.

The multi-dimensional nature of feedback adds a layer of complexity that you have likely experienced thus far in the playbook. Yet the result is worth it! To review where we have been so far, take a moment and try out this next task.

On the right is a list of words or concepts addressed thus far in the playbook. Using this list, construct a response to the question *how does feedback work?*

How does feedback work?

Key words or concepts:

Feed-up

Feed-back

Feed-forward

Give

Receive

Integrate

Where are we going?

How are we going?

Where are we going next?

Foundational Elements

Care

Take a moment to reflect on your learning. How are you progressing? Where do you need to spend a little more time in this module?

Consider these questions to guide your self-reflection and self-assessment:

1. Can I explain the four components of credibility?

2. Can I connect credibility with the three triggers that disrupt the feedback loop?

3. Can I identify specific strategies that foster, nurture, and sustain credibility for each member of our school and classroom community?

4. Can I explain how credibility supports the feedback loop?

Access videos and other resources at
resources.corwin.com/howfeedbackworks.

8

HOW IMPORTANT IS *CLARITY* IN HOW FEEDBACK WORKS?

LEARNING INTENTION

We are learning about clarity and the importance clarity plays in how feedback works.

SUCCESS CRITERIA

We have successfully completed this module when

1. We can identify the role each of the first three Cs plays in how feedback works.

2. We can explain what is meant by clarity from both our perspective and our learners' perspective.

3. We can identify how clarity guides different aspects of feedback.

4. We can find additional resources to support the establishing and sharing of clarity in our own schools and classrooms.

Care and **credibility** set the foundation for **who** is giving, receiving, and integrating the feedback. Quality professional relationships allow both the giver and receiver to view each other with mutual trust and respect. When that relationship aligns with the credibility of **who** is giving, receiving, and integrating the feedback, the feedback loop has the potential to work at the highest level of efficiency and effectiveness. Now we will turn our attention to the substance of the feedback. The C we are unpacking in this module is **clarity**. **Clarity** provides the foundation for **what** is given, received, and integrated into where we are going next in our teaching and learning.

Video 8.1: Introduction to Module 8

resources.corwin.com/ howfeedbackworks

Care and credibility set the foundation for **who** is giving, receiving, and integrating the feedback.

Clarity sets the foundation for **what** feedback is given, received, and integrated.

Communication sets the foundation for **how** the feedback is given.

Take a moment to write down your response to the following question. How do you know what the feedback should be? In other words, feedback about what?

Clarity tells us the substance of the feedback. When asked what the feedback should be about, the answer depends solely on clarity. So, what is **clarity**?

CLARITY ABOUT LEARNING, FOR FEEDBACK

The concept of clarity is exactly as the name suggests: Are teachers and learners clear about the teaching and learning in their school or classroom? As you also may have guessed, clarity is not as simple as the previous sentence suggests. Let's look at two examples before connecting the idea of clarity with how feedback works.

>>> Example 1

Learners enter Room 119, Ms. Michaels' biology class. Ms. Michaels greets each of them as they enter the room, asking a few of them questions about last night's soccer game or the upcoming Trivia Night hosted by the Academic Booster's Club. As the second bell rings, signaling the start of the block, Ms. Michaels directs their attention to the board where she has listed out the tasks for the day. "Good morning, folks. Today, we have quite a list to knock out to get through the standard focusing on cellular processes. Take a look." On the board is the following list of tasks:

1. Read Section 7–1 introducing you to Cellular Respiration.

2. Watch and complete the Nearpod for today.

3. Finish up the study guide for Friday's test.

4. If there is remaining time, use that time to work on the Cell Model Project.

Without much of a fuss, the learners get busy working on the tasks for the day.

Using the space provided, write down your thoughts and reactions to this example. What are your immediate impressions of Ms. Michaels' start to the class period?

We will return to each of these two examples in just a moment. For now, we are just generating our thoughts and reactions to this example.

》》》 Example 2

Across the hall from Ms. Michaels' classroom is Mr. Otto's biology class. Mr. Otto also greets his students as they enter the classroom, asking them about their day, commenting on specific extracurricular events, and complimenting them on their outfit or new haircut. However, the ringing of the second bell is where the differences between these two classrooms emerge. Mr. Otto quickly grabs their attention and directs them to a question on the board that reads, "What happens when I get dehydrated, and why does it matter?" After he reads the question to his learners, he allows them time to talk among themselves about dehydration and their initial responses to the question. During this conversation, he is recording their responses, use of vocabulary, and ideas. He uses this information to transition to the focus of the day's learning. "Today, we are learning about cellular respiration and its importance to us and other living organisms."

Before moving into the learning experience, he shares the success criteria with his learners both verbally and on the board.

"By the end of today, you will be able to describe the process of cellular respiration, list the chemical equations of cellular respiration, and explain the importance of cellular respiration to us as humans. In fact, you will be able to answer our guiding question for the day. Let's get started."

From there, Mr. Otto introduces the learning experiences and tasks for the day.

Using the space provided, write down your thoughts and reactions to this example. What are your immediate impressions of Mr. Otto's start to the class period?

Before connecting this to how feedback works, let's unpack these two examples. You likely noticed that one classroom focused on what learners were supposed to do, while the other classroom focused on what learners were supposed to learn. Rather than using an agenda like Ms. Michaels, Mr. Otto focused on the learning outcomes. While a visible schedule or agenda is an important tool for many learners, an agenda or task list is supplemental to clarity about the day's learning, the relevance or purpose of that learning, and the criteria for success. Whether presented at the start of the learning experience or after an initial task, the what, why, and how should be clear to both us and our learners.

Notice we said the what, why, and how should be clear to both us and our learners. Teacher clarity and student clarity are two sides of the same coin. In your classroom, are learners aware and able to articulate answers to the following three questions (Fisher et al., 2016):

1. What am I learning?
2. Why am I learning this?
3. How will I know if I am successful?

For this to happen, we must walk into each class day with the following three questions answered for ourselves:

1. What do I want my students to learn?
2. Why am I asking them to learn this?
3. How will I know they have learned it?

The power of these three questions cannot be overstated. Do a quick self-assessment on the presence of these three questions in your own school or classroom.

Use the space provided in the chart to reflect on how your learners would respond to these questions. Would they answer them consistently? Which question would be more challenging than the others? What could you do to improve their answers to these questions? Engage in the same self-assessment for the teacher clarity questions.

Teacher Clarity	How would you respond to these questions each day?	Student Clarity	How would your students respond?
What do I want my students to learn?		What am I learning?	
Why am I asking my students to learn this?		Why am I learning this?	
How will I know if they have learned it?		How will I know if I am successful?	

Again, the power of these three questions cannot be overstated. Clarity around both sets of questions—teacher clarity and student clarity—drives the rest of the learning experience. In the original research study, Fendick (1990) describes four practices that come with clarity:

Clarity around the learning guides both us and our learners in the substance of the feedback.

1. **Clarity of organization:** Lesson tasks, assignments, and activities include links to the objectives and outcomes of learning (what we call learning intentions and success criteria).

2. **Clarity of explanation:** Information is relevant, accurate, and comprehensible to students.

3. **Clarity of examples and guided practice:** The lesson includes information that is illustrative and illuminating as students gradually move to independence, making progress with less support from the teacher.

4. **Clarity of assessment of student learning:** The teacher is regularly seeking out and acting upon the feedback they receive from students, especially through their verbal and written responses.

However, our research has uncovered a fifth practice that comes from having teacher clarity and student clarity. We want you to finish this statement by filling in the missing word.

Teacher clarity and student clarity allow for clarity of _____.

(Hint: The missing word is the focus of this entire playbook.)

Without clarity, feedback will not work. Clarity around the learning guides both us and our learners in the substance of the feedback. What feedback should we give, receive, and integrate? The answer depends on the what, why, and how of the learning experience for that day. Return to our two examples at the beginning of this module. Use the space below to describe the substance of the feedback you would expect to see in both Ms. Michaels' and Mr. Otto's biology class.

	Ms. Michaels' Biology Class	Mr. Otto's Biology Class
What feedback would you expect to observe?		

If you found it difficult to answer this question for Ms. Michaels' class, that is exactly the point. Clarity is foundational for feedback. One part of our answer to *how feedback works* must include clarity about the learning. The feedback we would expect to give, receive, and integrate is directly linked to the learning intention and success criteria created and shared by Mr. Otto. The chart below provides a better analysis of these two classrooms.

Ms. Michaels' Agenda	Potential Feedback
"Today, we have quite a list to knock out to get through the standard focusing on cellular processes. Take a look." 1. Read Section 7–1 introducing you to Cellular Respiration. 2. Watch and complete the Nearpod for today. 3. Finish up the study guide for Friday's test. 4. If there is remaining time, use that time to work on the Cell Model Project.	The feedback here would be focused on student behaviors. Are they reading Section 7–1; did they complete the Nearpod? Are they done with the study guide, and are they working on the Cell Model Project? Giving, receiving, and integrating feedback about the learning behind cellular respiration would be very difficult because "successful" learning is not clearly articulated by Ms. Michaels or the learners.
Mr. Otto's Guiding Question, Learning Intention, and Success Criteria	**Potential Feedback**
"What happens when I get dehydrated and why does it matter? "Today, we are learning about cellular respiration and its importance to us and other living organisms. "By the end of today, you will be able to 1. Describe the process of cellular respiration. 2. List the chemical equations of cellular respiration. 3. Explain the importance of cellular respiration to us as humans."	The feedback given, received, and integrated should be directly linked to the learning intention and success criteria. Specifically, the verbs of the success criteria. Feedback in Mr. Otto's class would focus on the learners' descriptions of the cellular respiration process. What vocabulary are they using, how in-depth is the description, and what connections is the learner making to the guiding question? Feedback would also focus on the correct listing of the chemical equations. Are they balanced? Do they include the necessary elements? Finally, both learners and Mr. Otto would focus the feedback on the explanation of the importance of cellular respiration. Again, what vocabulary are they using, how in-depth is the explanation, and what connections is the learner making to the guiding question?

Reflect on your own school or classroom. How do you establish clarity? Using the four practices that come with clarity (Fendick, 1990), use the space on the next page to reflect on your own teaching.

How do I establish and share what my students are expected to learn?

How do I make sure that learners know and understand what success looks like for the day's learning?

How do I make sure that the learning experience produces the evidence of learning?

How do I create assessments to check and monitor learners' progress?

While a comprehensive coverage of clarity is beyond the scope of this playbook, the following resources can support your learning journey in gaining and sharing clarity in your school or classroom:

➡ *Clarity for Learning* (Almarode & Vandas, 2013)

➡ *The Teacher Clarity Playbook, Grades K–12* (Fisher et al., 2018)

➡ *The Success Criteria Playbook* (Almarode et al., 2021)

Clarity begins with the teacher and involves

1. Unpacking the standard

2. Developing a learning progression

3. Constructing learning intentions and success criteria

4. Designing relevant, rigorous, and authentically engaged tasks

5. Creating checks for understanding to monitor learners' progress through the progression

6. Building assessments to identify learners' growth in learning

7. Sharing this with learners

Each one of these seven parts opens the door for feedback and guides the substance of that feedback. Let's look at four specific examples of learning intentions and success criteria. These provide clarity about the expectations of the learning experience or task. Use the space provided to describe where you would focus the feedback.

Learning Intentions	Examples of Success Criteria	Focus of the Feedback
Mathematics		
Eighth-Grade Mathematics We are learning about the differences between surface area and volume.	We can distinguish between situations that are applications of surface area and those that are applications of volume. We can explain how the volume of a shape is affected by changing one of the dimensions. We can develop a mathematical model for multiplying the dimension of a shape by a given factor.	
Science		
High School Physics I am learning about the role of a net force on the motion of an object.	I can explain what is meant by a net force. I can determine the relative magnitude and direction of all forces acting on a system in a given situation. I can describe the motion of an object using vector quantities.	
English Language Arts		
First-Grade Language Arts I am learning that editing helps make my writing better.	I can identify areas in my writing that need editing. I can use the tools available to me to help edit my writing. I can give feedback to my writing buddy. I can share my writing with others.	

(Continued)

(Continued)

Learning Intentions	Examples of Success Criteria	Focus of the Feedback
Social Studies		
High School United States History We are learning about the impact of territorial expansion on the United States.	We can identify major territorial expansions of the 1800s. We can explain how these expansions affected the political map of the United States. We can explain how different factors influenced the territorial expansion of the United States.	

Our focus in this module is that clarity is foundational to how feedback works. Return to the previous modules of this playbook. Let's spend some time connecting clarity with our previous learning. In the space below, describe how clarity, knowing the what, why, and how of the day's learning, is foundational to other concepts in this playbook. We have provided a few examples to get you started.

Prior Learning	How is this concept supported by clarity?
Feed-up	
Feed-back	
Feed-forward	

Prior Learning	How is this concept supported by clarity?
Giving	**Example:** For the teacher, the feedback given should only focus on the success criteria and avoid extraneous information. For example, if the verb in the success criteria is *describe*, the feedback given should focus on the description, not the learner's handwriting or choice of writing utensil.
Receiving	
Integrating	
Care	**Example:** Setting clear and high expectations communicates to our learners that we believe they can do it. In addition, clear expectations lessen the stress and anxiety of not knowing what is expected. As Brené Brown says, "Clear is kind." This goes a long way in quality professional relationships.
Credibility	

Clarity is an essential part of making feedback work. By having answers to the three questions—what, why, and how—we have insight into the substance of the feedback given, received, and integrated. **Care** and **credibility** only get us so far. The content of the feedback exchanged in our schools and classrooms should move us forward in the learning progression. However, if that learning progression and the steps within that progression are not clearly defined, feedback can turn into empty statements that chip away at the **care** and **credibility** we have worked to establish. Without clarity, we may unconsciously put up one or more of the three feedback blockers from Module 5. As we close out this module, take a moment to identify how a lack of clarity can trigger feedback blockers.

Feedback Blocker	How is this triggered by a lack of clarity?
Identity trigger	
Truth trigger	
Relationship trigger	

Take a moment to reflect on your learning. How are you progressing? Where do you need to spend a little more time in this module?

Consider these questions to guide your self-reflection and self-assessment:

1. Can I identify the role each of the first three Cs plays in how feedback works?

2. Can I explain what is meant by clarity from both our perspective and our learners' perspective?

3. Can I identify how clarity guides different aspects of feedback?

4. Can I find additional resources to support the establishing and sharing of clarity in our own schools and classroom?

Access videos and other resources at
resources.corwin.com/howfeedbackworks.

9

WHAT IS THE ROLE OF EVIDENCE IN HOW FEEDBACK WORKS?

LEARNING INTENTION

We are learning about the importance of evidence of learning in supporting the feedback loop.

SUCCESS CRITERIA

We have successfully completed this module when

1. We can connect the generation of evidence to giving, receiving, and integrating feedback.

2. We can identify strategies that generate evidence of learning.

3. We can use our own lesson plans to develop sources of evidence that will guide the contents of the feedback loop.

We have looked at three of the Cs that are foundational for feedback. Let's review the role they play in supporting feedback. On the next page, fill in the missing words (*how*, *who*, and *what*).

Video 9.1: Introduction to Module 9

resources.corwin.com/ howfeedbackworks

Care and **credibility** set the foundation for _____ is giving, receiving, and integrating the feedback.

Clarity sets the foundation for _____ feedback is given, received, and integrated.

Communication sets the foundation for _____ the feedback is given.

We are not quite done with clarity. When we establish and share clarity about the learning, we gain understanding about the content of the feedback, what the feedback should be about. Turn back to pages 103–104 where you were asked to describe the focus of the feedback based on the learning intentions and success criteria. Review your responses to get ready for the next steps in this module.

Ms. Weatherly is a high school history teacher. In fact, she is the teacher who established and shared the learning intention and success criteria from the previous module.

Learning Intention	Success Criteria
We are learning about the impact of territorial expansion on the United States.	We can identify major territorial expansions of the 1800s. We can explain how these expansions affected the political map of the United States. We can explain how different factors influenced the territorial expansion of the United States.

As you correctly described in the previous module, the focus of the feedback for this particular learning experience should be on learners' capacity to

1. Identify major territorial expansions of the 1800s.

2. Explain how these expansions affected the political map of the United States.

3. Explain how different factors influenced the territorial expansion of the United States.

That's right, the success criteria are directly correlated with the focus of the feedback. If that is what successful learning looks like, then we should expect learners to give, receive, and integrate feedback that moves them closer to these outcomes. But we can't stop there. Consider the following scenarios or possible learning experiences implemented by Ms. Weatherly for these specific learning intentions and success criteria.

Example 1

Ms. Weatherly decides to begin today's class with a self-assessment. She provides her learners with the success criteria and, using a Likert scale, asks them to rate their level of comfort with that criterion. From there, she moves into a mini-lesson where her learners complete guided notes on the major territorial expansions of the United States in the 1800s. She is always moving around the room to monitor learners as they complete the fill-in notes. At the end of the mini-lesson, she asks her learners to revisit their self-assessment to see if they feel more comfortable with the success criteria. As a final exit task, learners participate in a Kahoot! about territorial expansions.

Using the space provided, write down your thoughts and reactions to this scenario. What are your immediate impressions of Ms. Weatherly's approach to the learning experience?

>>> Example 2

As the students file into Ms. Weatherly's class, she has a three-minute writing prompt on the board for learners to start as soon as they are settled in their desks. They know that they are to set their own timers and work on a response to the writing prompt for three minutes. Today's prompt is "Why would a country want to expand its territory?" After everyone has had a chance to write for three minutes, she asks her learners to share their responses with their shoulder partners and make any edits to their responses in a different color pen or marker. She moves around the room and listens to their responses. As she moves through the mini-lesson, she asks certain students to share their responses to highlight the key points in her mini-lesson. At certain spots in the lesson, she pauses and asks learners to fill in their guided notes. But instead of simply filling in facts, the fill-in notes are in the form of questions that they can answer with the help of their shoulder partners. At the end of class, she posts a QR code on the screen that directs learners to an exit ticket on their phones or laptops. The exit ticket takes the three success criteria and converts them into questions the students must answer:

1. List the major territorial expansions of the 1800s.

2. How did these expansions affect the political map of the United States?

3. What factors influenced the territorial expansion of the United States? How did they influence the territorial expansion?

Using the space provided on the next page, write down your thoughts and reactions to this scenario. What are your immediate impressions of Ms. Weatherly's second approach to the learning experience?

While there are many similarities and differences between these two possible options for Ms. Weatherly, we want to direct your attention to the success criteria for both options and the specific strategies selected and implemented in example 2. In both of these options, the learners were working toward the same success criteria. However, in the second example, learners engaged in strategies that made their thinking visible. While clarity sets the foundation for what feedback is given, received, and integrated, there must be something about which feedback can be given, received, and integrated. In other words, when we make student thinking and learning visible, there is evidence of learning available for feedback.

> **Feedback works when evidence of learning is generated in the learning experience. This evidence should make thinking and learning visible to both us and our learners.**

If we do not generate evidence that is visible during the learning, we do not have any insight into what students are thinking, which decisions they make during the learning experience, why they make those decisions, and/or how they are making meaning of the content, skills, and understandings. When we do make their learning and thinking visible, we have insight into their thinking, decisions, and meaning making and evidence to back it up. Silent classrooms where learners can hide during the lesson do not allow feedback to work. What would you possibly give them feedback about other than their behavior?

Let's connect these dots together with Ms. Weatherly's options. First of all, you can now see that example 2 is the better of the two options for many reasons, not the least of which is making feedback work in her classroom. Second, we want to illustrate the relationship between her success criteria, choice of strategies, and the generation of evidence.

In the below chart, you see Ms. Weatherly's learning intention and success criteria are listed in the first column. In the second column, list the specific strategy or strategies that provide a source of evidence generated during the learning experience. Do the same for example 2 in the third column. If you cannot find a source of evidence in one of the options, simply leave the space blank or write "no evidence generated."

Learning Intention and Success Criteria	Source of Evidence	
Learning Intention We are learning about the impact of territorial expansion on the United States.	Option 1	Option 2
Success Criteria 1 We can identify major territorial expansions of the 1800s.	Option 1	Option 2
Success Criteria 2 We can explain how these expansions affected the political map of the United States.	Option 1	Option 2
Success Criteria 3 We can explain how different factors influenced the territorial expansion of the United States.	Option 1	Option 2

So, which option generated the most evidence for both Ms. Weatherly and her students to see their thinking and learning? Which option provided the most opportunity to give, receive, and integrate feedback?

In the space below, write the big idea presented on page 110 in this module. Yep, simply copy that statement from page 110 into the space below. This is to emphasize the importance of generating evidence for feedback.

Clarity, communicated through the learning intentions and success criteria, guides us toward the evidence to generate during the learning experience. The learning intentions and success criteria help us select the strategies that generate that evidence. Deciding which strategies to use in a learning experience can be difficult with so many possible options available to us. Do we use a think-pair-share here or will a forced-choice exit ticket work just as well? Do we use a jigsaw in today's learning experience or reciprocal teaching? What about a written summary or a verbal summary?

Let's return one more time to Ms. Weatherly's learning intention and success criteria. On page 108, locate the verbs used in the success criteria. Then write those verbs in the space below.

These three verbs point us in the direction of certain strategies and, at the same time, away from others. The verbs of the success criteria tell us the evidence we and our learners need to generate during the learning experience. They also tell us what the strategy should ask learners to do. For example, if Ms. Weatherly needs her learners to be able to explain how these expansions affected the political map of the United States, then she needs to look for and select a strategy that gives them the opportunity to explain. Below are several examples of strategies; circle the ones that give learners the opportunity to explain—and make their thinking and learning visible through their explanations.

> We can explain how these expansions affected the political map of the United States.

1. A Kahoot! or some other clicker-based task

2. Think-pair-share

3. Guided notes

4. Forced-choice check for understanding

5. Thumbs up, thumbs down review

6. Three-minute write

Hopefully, you selected option 2 and option 6. A think-pair-share and a three-minute write provide an opportunity for learners to explain. A think-pair-share is a verbal opportunity, and a three-minute write is a written opportunity. But this does not mean there is anything wrong with the other four options.

Consider Ms. Weatherly's first success criteria.

> We can identify major territorial expansions of the 1800s.

Now, which options provide the evidence needed for feedback? *All of them!* Let's apply this to the learning intentions and success criteria first presented in the previous module. The chart on the next page should look very familiar to you. These first two columns are the same as they were in Module 8. The third column is different. In Module 8, you were asked to reflect on the focus of the feedback in each of these learning experiences based on the learning intentions and success criteria. This time, we want you to list out specific strategies that would generate the evidence needed to provide that feedback. What are possible strategies that these teachers could select to make thinking and learning visible to both the teacher and the students? List as many as you can.

Learning Intentions	Examples of Success Criteria	Strategies for Generating Evidence
Mathematics		
Eighth-Grade Mathematics We are learning about the differences between surface area and volume.	We can distinguish between situations that are applications of surface area and those that are applications of volume. We can explain how the volume of a shape is affected by changing one of the dimensions. We can develop a mathematical model for multiplying the dimension of a shape by a given factor.	
Science		
High School Physics I am learning about the role of a net force on the motion of an object.	I can explain what is meant by a net force. I can determine the relative magnitude and direction of all forces acting on a system in a given situation. I can describe the motion of an object using vector quantities.	
English Language Arts		
First-Grade Language Arts I am learning that editing helps make my writing better.	I can identify areas in my writing that need editing. I can use the tools available to me to help edit my writing. I can give feedback to my writing buddy. I can share my writing with others.	
Social Studies		
High School United States History We are learning about the impact of territorial expansion on the United States.	We can identify major territorial expansions of the 1800s. We can explain how these expansions affected the political map of the United States. We can explain how different factors influenced the territorial expansion of the United States.	

One incredibly powerful finding about teaching and learning strategies is that the potential impact of strategies lies in how visible they make student thinking and learning. Put another way, those evidence-based practices that have the highest potential impact on learning all make student thinking and learning visible. For example, which teaching and learning strategy do you think has the highest effect size? Lecturing or classroom discussion?

The answer is classroom discussion, by far. The reason for this striking difference (lectures = −0.18; classroom discussion = 0.82) lies in the fact that one of these approaches provides visible evidence to both us and our students. This evidence allows us to give and receive feedback about that visible evidence and do something about it! There is actually something into which learners can integrate the feedback. For us, we integrate that feedback into our decisions about where to go next in the learning experience.

This is powerful. This is how feedback works.

Try applying this finding to other strategies. Below is a list of strategies. Use the chart to test out the finding that the most effective teaching and learning strategies make thinking and learning visible.

Strategy	Does it generate visible evidence?	Effect Size From www.visiblelearningmetax.com	Why? What potential evidence is generated?
Concept mapping	Yes or No		
Clickers	Yes or No		
Programmed instruction	Yes or No		
Teaching test taking	Yes or No		

(Continued)

(Continued)

Strategy	Does it generate visible evidence?	Effect Size From www.visiblelearningmetax.com	Why? What potential evidence is generated?
Outlining and summarizing	Yes or No		
Reciprocal teaching	Yes or No		
Cooperative learning	Yes or No		
Use of slide presentations	Yes or No		
One-to-one laptops	Yes or No		
Jigsaw	Yes or No		

Do you see the point? Evidence-generating strategies matter. They matter because they make thinking and learning visible. They matter because they give us evidence for getting, receiving, and integrating feedback.

To close out this module, we want you to apply this to your own teaching. Evidence generation is key to how feedback works.

Locate a recent lesson plan from a previous lesson and an upcoming lesson. Take a few moments and review both of those lesson plans.

Now, looking first at the previous lesson plan, review the learning intention and success criteria for this past lesson. Write the learning intention and success criteria in the first column of the chart just as we did with Ms. Weatherly's lesson.

Learning Intention and Success Criteria	Source of Evidence

In the second column, list the source of evidence generated during the learning experience. If you do not have a source of evidence, simply leave the space blank or write "no evidence generated."

How did you do? Did all of your learning intentions and success criteria have a source of evidence generated during the learning experience? Did some learning intentions and success criteria have more evidence than others?

Now, let's take this analysis and apply this thinking to an upcoming lesson of your own. In the following chart, record the learning intentions and success criteria for the upcoming lesson.

Learning Intention and Success Criteria	Source of Evidence

As we have done in the previous two tasks, list the source of evidence you currently plan to generate during the learning experience. Now, this time, if you do not have a source of evidence, how would you edit and revise your lesson plan to ensure that you do make thinking and learning visible around that particular outcome? Make this adjustment while you can!

Take a moment to reflect on your learning. How are you progressing? Where do you need to spend a little more time in this module?

Consider these questions to guide your self-reflection and self-assessment:

1. Can I connect the generation of evidence to giving, receiving, and integrating feedback?

2. Can I identify strategies that generate evidence of learning?

3. Can I use our own lesson plans to develop sources of evidence that will guide the contents of the feedback loop?

Access videos and other resources at
resources.corwin.com/howfeedbackworks.

10

WHAT ROLE DO TEACHER NOTICING AND STUDENT NOTICING PLAY IN HOW FEEDBACK WORKS?

LEARNING INTENTION

We are now learning about the practice of noticing and how noticing supports how feedback works.

SUCCESS CRITERIA

We have successfully completed this module when

1. We can define what is meant by teacher noticing and student noticing.

2. We can describe how teacher noticing and student noticing supports the feedback loop.

3. We can intentionally plan for noticing in our teaching and our students' learning.

Video 10.1: Introduction to Module 10

resources.corwin.com/ howfeedbackworks

This module is all about what we notice. You may be wondering, *what about the fourth C, communication?* We have not forgotten about that. It will be the focus of Module 12. But right now, we are lingering a bit longer on clarity and how noticing can help us clarify our own thinking and that of our students.

This is a rather fun topic because our eyes often play tricks on us when we are engaged in noticing. Take a look at the picture on the facing page. What do you see?

Image source: Wikimedia Commons.

> What do you see in this image? Jot down what you notice about this image.

Let's try another one.

Image source: Jastrow (1899).

> What do you see in this image? Jot down what you notice about this image.

The second image likely created a different response from you and, if you shared this with colleagues, from them as well. While the first image may have created a sense of uncertainty about the number of legs on the elephant, the second image created a different type of uncertainty. Did you see the head of a bird or the head of a rabbit?

What you noticed in the second image depended on how you approached the sketch.

Now, look at this painting on the next page of a shepherd looking over his sheep. Answer the following questions about the painting.

Image source: Courtesy of Oleg Shupliak.

How many sheep are in the painting?

_____

How many trees do you see? _____

How many different types of flowers do you see?

_____

Oh, did you happen to notice the face in the painting? Take another look and see if you recognize a man's face in the painting. The mustache is the shepherd's shirt. The windows in each of the two houses represent the eyes. The old trees on the left and right outline his face. Do you see it now?

Take a moment to summarize the point of these past three tasks. What do you believe is the point (or points) we are trying to make?

Noticing is an active process that involves multiple systems in our bodies. This is often referred to as attention and perception. When you first looked at images in this module, there were certain characteristics or features that you initially noticed, those that you noticed after viewing the picture for some time, and then those features that you noticed **only after someone pointed them out to you**. Using your experiences with these three images, use the space below to brainstorm some factors that influence what you initially notice, notice after some time, or never notice without a cue in viewing any image.

Your list likely contained factors like color, shading, or where your eyes landed first on the image. You may also have identified influences like prior knowledge, prior experiences, personal interests, and context. For example, if you were already familiar with any of these images (prior knowledge), that will influence what you notice in these images. If you have prior experiences or have a pet rabbit, that will influence what you notice in the second image. If you are standing next to a duck pond, that may play a role in what you notice as well.

However, there is one influence we want to make absolutely sure you have on the list: clarity! If *clarity* is not on your list, please go add it now in **BIG BOLD LETTERS**. If *clarity* is already on your list, please circle it or highlight the term.

After viewing the third image, you were asked a series of questions.

> *Oh, did you happen to notice the face in the painting? Take another look and see if you recognize a man's face in the painting. The mustache is the shepherd's shirt. The windows in each of the two houses represent the eyes. The old trees on the left and right outline his face. Do you see it now?*

This prompting gave you additional information, or clarity, about what you should notice in the image. That's right, when we are prompted or primed, we notice certain things over others. If you did not initially notice the face in the third image, you likely read the series of questions and used those prompting questions to then return to the image and integrate that into your noticing of the image. That is exactly how noticing works.

NOTICING

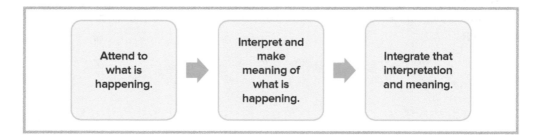

Now let's talk about what this has to do with feedback.

In our schools and classrooms, **noticing** is the active process of attending to what is happening during a learning experience, the interactions, or tasks; interpreting what we see; and then using that interpretation to decide where to go next (Schoenfeld, 2011). This concept of noticing applies to both teachers and learners. When we are engaged in noticing, we often engage in an internal dialogue about what is going on in our classroom.

Noticing by the teacher . . .	Noticing by the student . . .
What am I noticing about my learners as they engage in the learning experience?	What am I noticing about myself as I engage in the learning experience?
What are my students noticing as they engage in their learning experience?	What are my peers noticing as they engage with me in the learning experience?
What does this tell me about their current progress toward the learning intention and success criteria?	What does this tell me about my current progress toward the learning intention and success criteria?

Source: Adapted from Sherin et al. (2011).

What we want to notice and what we want our students to notice is communicated through our directions, gestures, body language, posters on the wall, models or objects on the demonstration table, the arrangement of the classroom, and our learning intentions and success criteria.

Clarity serves as a prompt that helps us and our students engage in successful **noticing** during a learning experience.

If clarity tells us what the feedback should be about, **teacher noticing and student noticing** are required to identify where that feedback should be given, received, and integrated.

To give feedback that works, we and our students must engage in noticing. That noticing includes

1. Recognizing what the learning intentions and success criteria are for the learning experience

2. Recognizing where the receiver of the feedback is relative to those learning intentions and success criteria

3. Recognizing the best way to give that feedback so that feedback blockers are not triggered and the feedback will be integrated into the next steps

Now it's your turn. To receive feedback that works, we and our students must engage in noticing. That noticing includes

1.

2.

3.

And finally, to integrate feedback, we and our students must engage in noticing. That noticing includes

1.

2.

3.

Take a look at page 12 in Module 1. You did not **notice** it at the time, but we planted the seed for this module way back then. From that point to right now, the word *notice* is used no fewer than 30 times in this playbook. In each of those situations, we were prompting you to recognize an important idea, major concept, or key detail in this playbook.

One of the roles in establishing and sharing clarity is that we have the lenses needed to notice where learners are making progress or not making progress toward the intended outcomes. We have the lenses needed to notice when and who our teaching is benefiting and when and who our teaching is not benefiting.

On the flip side, when our learners are clear on the three questions of clarity (write those three questions on the next page) they have the lens needed to notice their current level of understanding, where they are making progress, and where they needed additional learning. They have the lenses needed to frame their questions, give us feedback, receive our feedback, and integrate the feedback they are provided by us and their peers.

1.

2.

3.

This requires a high level of intentionality. However, we have adjusted the last column on the right (Module 1, page 15) to begin developing our noticing skills. Yes, we can develop noticing skills by pre-planning what we are looking for during the learning experience and anticipating student responses.

We can develop noticing skills by pre-planning what we are looking for during the learning experience and anticipating student responses.

Ms. Campbell is planning her unit on fictional text in reading. She has unpacked the standards and identified the major success criteria for this unit.

When reading fictional texts, students must be able to

1. Make and confirm predictions

2. Connect previous experiences to new texts

3. Ask and answer questions using the text for support

4. Describe characters, setting, and plot events in fiction and poetry

5. Identify the conflict and the resolution

6. Identify the theme

7. Summarize stories and events with beginning, middle, and end in the correct sequence

8. Draw conclusions based on the text

9. Read/reread familiar stories and poems with fluency, accuracy, and meaningful expression

Prior to implementing any learning experience during this unit, she develops her list of evidence that must be generated during the learning experiences. We did this in the previous module. Then, she develops a list of look-fors, things she is going to watch for and listen for during the learning experience. Several of the items on this list are areas that often challenge learners. Let's look at Ms. Campbell's success criteria for one learning intention.

Second-Grade Reading: Fictional Text			
		What would you be looking for?	
Learning Intention	Examples of Success Criteria	Look-Fors	Possible Challenges
We are learning about predictions and how they help me understand what I read.	I can make predictions when I read. I can share those predictions with my reading buddy. I can confirm my predictions using evidence from the text.	• Do they look at the title and pictures before they read? • Can they talk about their prediction using key vocabulary? • Can they ask and answer questions like "What do you think will happen next?" and "Why do you think so?"	• My learners often make off-the-cuff predictions without ever looking at the text. • They often back up their predictions with their life experiences and not evidence from the text. • They often ask fact-based questions.

Engaging in this brainstorming, Ms. Campbell is better prepared to notice the relevant aspects of the learning experience and less likely to get distracted, miss a key concept, skill, or understanding, and offer feedback that does not move the learner forward in this specific learning progression.

Likewise, her learners are less likely to attend to irrelevant details, miss a key concept, skill, or understanding, and receive and integrate feedback that does not move them forward in this specific learning progression.

Let's return to the examples of learning intentions and success criteria from the previous module. As you revisit these learning intentions and success criteria, imagine you were the classroom teacher—what would you be looking for during the learning experience?

Mathematics			
		What would you be looking for?	
Learning Intention	Examples of Success Criteria	Look-Fors	Possible Challenges
Eighth-Grade Mathematics We are learning about the differences between surface area and volume.	We can distinguish between situations that are applications of surface area and those that are applications of volume. We can explain how the volume of a shape is affected by changing one of the dimensions. We can develop a mathematical model for multiplying the dimension of a shape by a given factor.		

Science			
		What would you be looking for?	
Learning Intention	**Examples of Success Criteria**	**Look-Fors**	**Possible Challenges**
High School Physics I am learning about the role of a net force on the motion of an object.	I can explain what is meant by a net force. I can determine the relative magnitude and direction of all forces acting on a system in a given situation. I can describe the motion of an object using vector quantities.		

English Language Arts			
		What would you be looking for?	
Learning Intention	**Examples of Success Criteria**	**Look-Fors**	**Possible Challenges**
First-Grade Language Arts I am learning that editing helps make my writing better.	I can identify areas in my writing that need editing. I can use the tools available to me to help edit my writing. I can give feedback to my writing buddy. I can share my writing with others.		

Social Studies			
		What would you be looking for?	
Learning Intention	**Examples of Success Criteria**	**Look-Fors**	**Possible Challenges**
High School United States History We are learning about the impact of territorial expansion on the United States.	We can identify major territorial expansions of the 1800s. We can explain how these expansions affected the political map of the United States. We can explain how different factors influenced the territorial expansion of the United States.		

To close out this module, we want you to connect clarity, evidence generation, and noticing to your classroom.

Locate another pair of lesson plans: one from a recent lesson and one upcoming lesson. Take a few moments and review both of those lesson plans.

Now, looking first at the previous lesson plan, review the learning intention and success criteria for this past lesson (if you had them). Write the learning intention and success criteria in the first column of the chart; if you didn't have them, create them now. In the second column, list the source of evidence generated during the learning experience. Just as we did in Module 9, if you do not have a source of evidence, simply leave the space blank or write "no evidence generated."

To incorporate noticing into this task, use the third column to describe what you will be looking for in this evidence. Be as specific as possible. We have provided an example from the previous module to get you started. Now, grab your previous lesson plan and go to it!

Learning Intention and Success Criteria	Source of Evidence	What are you looking for in this evidence?
Success Criteria 2: We can explain how these expansions affected the political map of the United States.	1. Three-minute write 2. Conversations with shoulder partners 3. Edits and revisions made to the three-minute write 4. Questions during the guided notes 5. Response to "Can I?" question 2 on the exit ticket	I will be looking for the type of vocabulary utilized and the accuracy of that use. I will be looking for the connections they make between expansion and the political map. I will be looking for the clarity (flow and logic) of their explanation. I will be looking for both change and consistency in their thinking across all five sources of evidence.

Now, let's take this analysis and apply this thinking to an upcoming lesson. In the chart below, record the learning intentions and success criteria for the upcoming lesson. As we have done in the previous two tasks, list the source of evidence you currently plan to generate during the learning experience and what you will be looking for in this evidence. This time, if you do not have a source of evidence, how would you edit and revise your lesson plan to ensure that you do make thinking and learning visible around that particular outcome? Make this adjustment while you can!

Learning Intention and Success Criteria	Source of Evidence	What are you looking for in this evidence?

Take a deep breath. You have done great work! These last 10 modules have set us up for the exchange of feedback that moves learning forward. We have arrived at the location in our journey where "the rubber meets the road." How do we communicate the feedback we have clearly anticipated from our learning intentions, success criteria, evidence-generating strategies, and the anticipation of student responses?

Take a moment to reflect on your learning. How are you progressing? Where do you need to spend a little more time in this module?

Consider these questions to guide your self-reflection and self-assessment:

1. Can I define what is meant by teacher noticing and student noticing?

2. Can I describe how teacher noticing and student noticing supports the feedback loop?

3. Can I intentionally plan for noticing in our teaching and our students' learning?

Access videos and other resources at
resources.corwin.com/howfeedbackworks.

11

WHAT ARE THE SIMILARITIES AND DIFFERENCES BETWEEN THE FOUR TYPES OF FEEDBACK?

LEARNING INTENTION

We are learning about the four types of feedback so that we can better engage our learners in the feedback loop.

SUCCESS CRITERIA

We have successfully completed this module when

1. We can give examples of each of the four types of feedback from our own schools and classrooms.

2. We can compare and contrast the four different types of feedback.

3. We can evaluate each of the four types of feedback on their effectiveness in moving learning forward.

4. We can explain the role of praise in student learning.

Video 11.1: Introduction to Module 11

resources.corwin.com/howfeedbackworks

We have arrived at the fourth and final C, **communication**. Over the past 10 modules, we have developed a definition of feedback, explored the different aspects of feedback, walked through the feedback loop, identified feedback blockers, and established the four foundational elements for how feedback works. While **care**, **credibility**, and **clarity** are essential and necessary for how feedback works, the communication of feedback is where the action happens in our schools and classrooms.

> Care and credibility are all about **who** is giving, receiving, and integrating the feedback.
>
> Clarity is all about **what** is being given, received, and integrated (i.e., the substance of the feedback).
>
> Communication is **how** feedback is given, received, and integrated.

As teachers, we are very interested in **how** to give, receive, and integrate feedback so that it works in moving teaching and learning forward. This is what we seek to do on a daily basis with our learners. Because this is the focus of a significant number of the decisions we make and actions we take in our schools and classrooms, communicating feedback will make up the remaining six modules of this playbook. Starting with the different types of feedback, we will look at how best to package those different types of feedback. Finally, we will look at specific examples of practices that communicate feedback that works.

To get us started, take a look at the following examples of feedback given to learners.

1. "Juan, you are an outstanding artist."

2. "The answer to number 7 is not 3. Take another look at that problem."

3. "You use this word several times in the same paragraph. How could you avoid this redundancy in your writing?"

4. Shanda reflects on her writing and asserts that "there is something missing in this transition. I don't think the reader can see the transition from this part to that part."

5. "Your supporting details are well-aligned with your thesis statement. Well done."

6. "Valerie, where could you locate an example of this type of chemical reaction? Have a look at the example and see if that helps your thinking."

7. "You have the process reversed. Try that again."

8. "Samantha, you are such a gifted writer."

9. "Your claim is not supported by evidence from the text. What could you add to your writing to support your strong claim?"

10. "Take a look at your shading. Is your shading consistent throughout your entire still life sketch?"

11. Denzel says to his shoulder partner, "Wait, this answer does not seem reasonable. Let's go back over our steps to this problem."

12. "Baxter, you did a great job today."

What did you notice (there's that word again) about these 12 examples of feedback? These 12 examples were overheard in a school and have many similarities and many differences. Use the space below to jot down your reflections about these examples.

Not all feedback is the same.

Beyond care, credibility, and clarity, if we do not communicate feedback well, the information can be lost in translation. This can diminish the impact of the feedback loop on the next steps in teaching and learning. If not all feedback is the same, what are the different types of feedback?

TYPES OF FEEDBACK

The consensus in the research is that there are four types of feedback (Hattie & Timperley, 2007):

1. Self or praise

2. Task

3. Process

4. Self-regulation

Before we dive into each type of feedback, what do you think distinguishes each type of feedback from the others?

What do think self-feedback or praise is? Give one or two examples.

What do think task feedback is? Illustrate your thinking with a few examples.

What do think process feedback is? Give some examples.

What is self-regulation feedback? What do you think this would look like in your classroom?

Hold on to your responses in the above boxes. We will revisit them shortly to edit and revise your answers.

Because feedback is most effective when we receive the feedback and integrate it into where we are going next in teaching and learning, it is critical that the feedback is communicated in a way that aligns with where we are in our teaching and learning journey. Of the four types of feedback, research has indicated that only three of the types of feedback are supportive of learning: *task, process,* and *self-regulation* (see Brummelman et al., 2013). Furthermore, the timing in the use of each type of feedback is dependent on the learning intentions, success criteria, and where we are in the learning journey (i.e., just starting out to being highly proficient).

Below is a continuum that represents progress toward proficiency in any concept, skill, or understanding. This continuum applies to us in our own professional learning, as well as learners in our schools and classrooms.

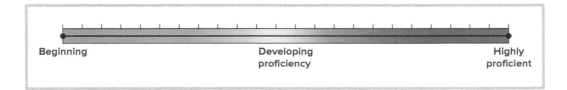

Beginning   Developing proficiency   Highly proficient

Where would you place task, process, and self-regulation feedback on that continuum? In other words, where on the continuum do you think task feedback is most effective? Process? Self-regulation?

Now, we know we have not even unpacked the different types of feedback. That is actually the point of these tasks. After we do, we will return to our initial responses to the continuum and the questions on page 136 to edit and revise our thinking.

So, here we go!

TASK FEEDBACK

As we initially engage in new learning, *task feedback* develops and supports our initial understanding of content and skills. Task feedback is corrective, precise, and focused on the accuracy of the content and skills within the learning experience. Task feedback communicates right, wrong, yes, no, do this, don't do that. As learners, we all rely on task feedback to add structure to concepts, ideas, terms, skills, and practices. The communication of this type of feedback can take the form of examples and non-examples, as well as explanations of procedural steps, key features, and context.

Examples of Task Feedback

1. **Accuracy.** "Joey, the answer to number 14 is wrong. Take another look at the way you balanced the equations. You have two coefficients that are not correct."

2. **Example and Non-Example.** "Georges Seurat's painting *A Sunday Afternoon on the Island of LaGrande Jatte* is an example of pointillism. This is different from tattooing. Let's compare the two."

3. **Procedural Steps.** "The steps for simplifying an expression are grouping symbols, exponents, multiplication/division from left to right, and then, addition/subtraction from left to right."

4. **Key Features.** "Remember, sonnets are 14 lines and follow either an ABBA ABBA CDE CDE rhyme scheme or, if you are writing a Shakespearean sonnet, ABAB CDCD EFEF GG."

5. **Context.** "We only reverse the inequality sign when we divide by a negative number."

Task feedback provides clear information to us and our learners about the parameters for what is or is not an aspect of the concept, idea, term, skill, or practice. Notice after each of the examples above, if the feedback is received and integrated, learners will have a clearer picture of a specific concept, idea, skill, or practice.

Now that we have defined task feedback, let's use this information as feedback for our responses at the opening of this module.

1. Return to your initial examples of feedback on page 134 and place a **T** next to those statements you believe are examples of task feedback.

2. Then, revisit your initial description of task feedback on page 136. What revisions or edits would you make to that response?

3. Finally, in the space below, list all the ways you provide task feedback to your learners. How do you get your own task feedback from colleagues or students?

PROCESS FEEDBACK

Process feedback is critical as we explore the why and the how of specific content, skills, and understandings. Process feedback moves us deeper into the learning. For process feedback to work, learners have likely identified clear boundaries between concepts and have developed an awareness of examples and non-examples, procedural steps, key features, and context associated with specific concepts, ideas, skills, or practices. In our initial learning, we strive to integrate task feedback into our learning to develop a strong foundation of concepts and skills. But we cannot stop there in the learning progression. We want to move beyond examples and non-examples, procedural steps, key features, and context.

As learners begin to develop proficiency with specific concepts, ideas, skills, or practices, the feedback should increasingly shift to process feedback. Whether from us or their peers, learners should receive feedback on their thinking, not just the accuracy of their responses. For example, teachers might engage students in further dialogue about the use of figurative language to convey an author's purpose: "Remember, the use of a simile or metaphor is an intentional and purposeful decision by the author. What is the author's purpose in this example?" This feedback does not tell students that they are right or wrong. Instead, the feedback, often in the form of a question, asks students to think about the process by which they determined the author's purpose in using figurative language.

> **Learners should receive feedback on their thinking, not just the accuracy of their responses.**

Examples of Process Feedback

1. "Joey, why is it important that we balance the chemical equations? What role do the coefficients play in understanding why some reactions are limited?"

2. "What do you notice about this painting and the decisions the artist appears to have made in creating this piece of art? What does this remind you of in today's world?"

3. "If you and I get different answers when we simplify the same expression, how do we know which one is correct? What might help ensure that we arrive at the same answer?"

4. "What is the rhyming scheme of this poem? How does that help you understand the context of the poem? What information is communicated through that rhyming scheme?"

5. "How is this problem different from the previous problem? Did you treat the inequality sign the same in both problems?"

Process feedback supports making connections, the use of multiple strategies, self-explanation, self-monitoring, self-questioning, and critical thinking. For example, a teacher may ask learners what strategies they used in making the calculations for a number of math problems and ask whether the strategy worked well or whether a different strategy may be more efficient. During a social studies lesson, a teacher may ask a student if primary or secondary sources were used to generate the historical inferences included in the student's essay and if the difference in the type of source might affect the accuracy of the inference. Rather than focusing on the correct answer regarding the relationship between an independent and dependent variable, a teacher may ask a student, "What is your explanation for your answer?" The focus of process feedback is on relationships between ideas and students' strategies for evaluating the reasonableness of an answer or solution. Process feedback enables students to explicitly learn from mistakes and helps learners identify different strategies for addressing a task.

Process feedback should support our capacity to engage in self-regulation feedback. That is, it should deepen thinking, reasoning, explanations, and connections. Do we prompt our learners through strategic questioning related to the learning process? What appears to be wrong, and why? What approach or strategies did the learner use or apply to the task? What is an explanation for the answer, response, or solution? What are the relationships with other parts of the task?

Let's use our new learning on process feedback as, well, as feedback for our responses at the opening of this module.

1. Return to your initial examples of feedback on page 134 and place a **P** next to those statements you believe are examples of process feedback.

2. Then, revisit your initial description of process feedback on page 136. What revisions or edits would you make to that response?

3. Finally, in the space below, list all the ways you provide process feedback to your learners. How do you get your own process feedback from colleagues or students?

SELF-REGULATION FEEDBACK

Self-regulation feedback refers to learners' ability to know what to do when they approach a new and different problem, are stuck, or have to apply their understanding in a new way. When we have reached a deep level of conceptual understanding and are armed with multiple strategies or processes, we are ready to self-regulate our own feedback.

Self-regulation feedback guides us in what to do when we don't know what to do, and the teacher is not in the room.

This promotes the transfer of learning to more rigorous tasks. Highly proficient learners are both ready for and benefit from self-regulation feedback. However, self-regulation feedback is not the only type of feedback that is important to these learners. For example, when we detect a misconception, or when a gap arises in foundational or background learning, learners still benefit from both task and process feedback. However, most of the feedback at this part of the learning process should be self-regulation through metacognition. Our role, as the teacher in the feedback at this level, is to ask questions to prompt further metacognition.

Eventually, learners practice metacognition independently through self-verbalization, self-questioning, and self-reflection. They take personal ownership of their learning, which provides increased motivation and understanding. The ability to think about our own thinking promotes self-awareness, enables us to problem solve around the learning task, and helps us understand what we need to do to meet the learning outcomes for the specific learning experience. To reiterate, self-regulation feedback means learners know what to do when they get stuck, when a new challenge arises, or when their teacher may not be available.

Examples of Self-Regulation Feedback

1. The teacher overhears Joey say, "Wait a minute. The law of conservation of mass says we cannot have more atoms on one side than we have on the other. Something is wrong. We have to go back and check our coefficients and subscripts."

2. A student in art history shares, "These paintings look very similar in style. But they cannot be from the same artist. What were the key features for pointillism again? That is where we need to start."

3. A math teacher observes that several students are stuck on multiple problems in this week's independent practice work. However, she notices that Alfonzo has grabbed his interactive math notebook and is working through the examples again. He is actually placing the examples next to the problem set and comparing and contrasting them.

4. As her English 12 students begin their independent analysis of a poem, the teacher watches several of them use the lettering technique she taught them to identify the rhyming scheme for each poem.

5. Before turning in today's exit ticket, Isabella goes over each inequality and checks her decision making. Prior to today's class, she developed a step-by-step process from her notes that she uses to double-check her work.

When we or our learners engage in self-regulation feedback, there is clear knowledge about our location in the learning process, knowledge about how we are progressing to or beyond the learning intention and success criteria, and we can monitor that progress. Yet there is still a need for scaffolding as we progress toward this metacognitive awareness. To develop metacognitive skills, we need to develop the capacity for self-questioning. We must model this through the questions we pose to students as students move from process feedback to self-regulation.

Let's use our new learning on self-regulation feedback as, well, as feedback for our responses at the opening of this module.

1. Return to your initial examples of feedback on page 134 and place an **S** next to those statements you believe are examples of process feedback.

2. Then, revisit your initial description of self-regulation feedback on page 136. What revisions or edits would you make to that response?

3. Finally, in the space below, list all the ways you provide self-regulation feedback to your learners. How do you engage in self-regulation feedback? Be specific.

Before we move into the closing task for this module, return to your continuum on page 137. Make sure you are satisfied with where you placed each type of feedback on that continuum. Remember, those learners that are highly proficient in specific content, skills, and understandings still benefit from task and process feedback. Maybe there is not just one type of feedback for each spot benchmark on the continuum.

WHAT ABOUT PRAISE?

As we close out this module, we want to spend just a moment on the idea that praise is not on the list of feedback that moves learning forward. This is both tough to hear and hard to make sense of in our schools and classrooms. The reason praise is not associated with moving learning forward has more to do with what it communicates. The examples from page 134 that reflect praise are repeated in the box below. What do these three statements communicate?

> 1. "Juan, you are an outstanding artist."
>
> 8. "Samantha, you are such a gifted writer."
>
> 12. "Baxter, you did a great job today."

These three statements communicate that the progress made by Juan, Samantha, and Baxter is intrinsic to them as human beings. Their art, writing, and overall behaviors are innate in them as human beings. In other words, Juan is naturally an outstanding artist—not that he is successful because of his time, effort, and work in developing his skills as an artist. This undercuts the process of learning and the progress made by Juan.

Furthermore, what happens when Juan is challenged by a particular piece of artwork? Is he suddenly not a good artist? Is Samantha suddenly not a good writer if she struggles to find the right words for her next poem? Is Baxter somehow not a good student if he makes a different decision on the playground today?

To be clear, we are not equating praise with giving kind, compassionate, and positive feedback to learners. That is not it at all. What we are saying is that feedback works when the information given, received, and integrated answers the three key questions for feedback (write those in the spaces below):

1.

2.

3.

How could we adjust statements 1, 8, and 12 so that they do answer the three questions? We will do the first one for you. Then, you revise the other two.

Praise	Revised to Effective Feedback
"Juan, you are an outstanding artist."	**Task:** "Juan, you have clearly developed your horizon line and remained consistent with your perspective and shading." **Process:** "How could you use additional color to communicate the emotion you are conveying through the guitar player?" **Self-Regulation:** Juan responds, "I think that my use of red and orange is too abrupt. I am going to fade these two colors together."
"Samantha, you are such a gifted writer."	**Task:** **Process:** **Self-Regulation:**
"Baxter, you did a great job today."	**Task:** **Process:** **Self-Regulation:**

With the four types of feedback in our toolkit, let's talk about how to package this feedback so that the feedback is well-received and integrated. We are on to Module 12.

Take a moment to reflect on your learning. How are you progressing? Where do you need to spend a little more time in this module?

Consider these questions to guide your self-reflection and self-assessment:

1. Can I give examples of each of the four types of feedback from our own schools and classrooms?

2. Can I compare and contrast the four different types of feedback?

3. Can I evaluate each of the four types of feedback on their effectiveness in moving learning forward?

4. Can I explain the role of praise in student learning?

Access videos and other resources at
resources.corwin.com/howfeedbackworks.

12

HOW SHOULD FEEDBACK BE COMMUNICATED?

LEARNING INTENTION

We are learning about key components of feedback delivery so that we can communicate that feedback effectively in our schools and classrooms.

SUCCESS CRITERIA

We have successfully completed this module when

1. We can identify key components of communicating feedback.

2. We can compare and contrast different ways to communicate feedback.

3. We can analyze our own communication of feedback across these key components.

4. We can relate the components of communicating feedback to the feedback loop.

Video 12.1: Introduction to Module 12

resources.corwin.com/howfeedbackworks

From the beginning of this playbook, we have defined *feedback* as the exchange of evaluative or corrective information about an action, event, or process and as the basis for improvement (Merriam-Webster, 2022). The overall goal of this exchange is to provide us and our students guidance about where to direct their time, energy, and effort in moving forward in their learning journey. Feedback only supports learning when the information is received and effectively integrated into where we are going next. To effectively integrate feedback into learning, the feedback must be received by us or our learners. To increase the likelihood that feedback is received and has an impact on increasing learning, feedback must address three very important questions for both the teacher and the learners (Hattie, 2012). As a quick review, write those three questions in the following box.

1.

2.

3.

Yet, the packaging matters. In other words, how these three questions are answered can and should vary depending on the situation. Let's return to the four reflective questions on page 25 in Module 3. Flip back and devote extra attention to questions 2 and 3. Write those questions in the box but contextualize them based on your own personal experiences. We have provided an example from our own conversations.

Our Example for Question 3: If I want to give them feedback on their research papers, how do I give that feedback so that they use it and don't simply toss my comments aside?

Think about several exchanges of feedback between you, your colleagues, and your learners. What prevented them from integrating the feedback into their learning? Use the three questions above and jot down some possible reasons why your feedback may not have been received and integrated into where they are going next. Then, think about the feedback you have received about your own work. What are some of the reasons you don't integrate feedback from others into where you are going next?

As you uncovered in the previous modules, feedback has a powerful impact on learning. For feedback to work, we and our learners must have clarity about

➡ The expectations of the learning experience

➡ The current level of performance for us and our learners

➡ Actions that we and our learners can take to close the gap

Feedback should be customized to support learners in closing the gap between their current location on their own learning progressions.

The giving, receiving, and integrating of feedback is designed to move us closer to the learning expectations. They are given to learners so that they know where to go next in their learning and received by us to make decisions about where to go next in our instruction. Then, the feedback given and received should specifically target what learners are expected to say and do to demonstrate that they have met the expectations of the learning experience or task (i.e., clarity through learning intentions and success criteria). This feedback should be customized to support learners in closing the gap between their current location on their own learning progressions. And finally, this feedback should provide insight into where more time, energy, and attention are needed to move that learning forward.

In the previous task, you looked at reasons why you or your learners did not integrate feedback into their next steps. Now consider times when you or they did integrate feedback. What are the similarities and differences between these two situations?

To be very honest, sometimes the substance (i.e., clarity) of the feedback is not the problem. Sometimes, care and credibility are not issues in the feedback. This leaves only one possibility: the packaging. The packaging of the feedback matters. For example, too much feedback, too fast, won't last. What if the feedback is provided verbally and the learner doesn't interpret the feedback the way you intended? What if the feedback is provided to the whole class, but some learners assume the information is not for them? Let's turn our attention to the variety of ways that we can give and receive feedback in the classroom.

Focus on learning, not the individual. Feedback works when the focus is on the learning and not the individual participating in the learning. Here's an example: "My explanation of net force and how it impacts the motion of an object needs improving, not me as a person. My solution to the mathematics problem is wrong, but I am not a wrong person. My writing is not clear, but I am not a bad writer. My understanding of the historical timeline is fuzzy, but I am not stupid." In each of those examples, the feedback was directed at the task and not the learner.

Take a look at these examples. Put a check by those that focus on the learning.

1.　"You are a great writer."

2.　"Take a look at the second paragraph. Where could you add a few supporting details to back up the claim in the opening paragraph?"

3.　"You are not getting similes and metaphors."

4.　"Take a moment to review the examples of similes and metaphors. Tell me what you notice about those examples."

5.　"You are not very athletic."

6.　"Remember, our overhand throwing cues are *T, L, step and throw.*"

7. "You are wrong, that is not one of the expansion territories."

8. "West Virginia is not one of the expansion territories."

Hopefully, a pattern emerged as you read through these examples. The even-numbered examples provided feedback on learning and thus increased the chances of the feedback being received by the learner.

General statements are often not received and integrated because almost everyone listening believes we are not talking to them.

➡️ **Feedback also needs to be "just-in-time, just-for-me information** delivered when and where it can do the most good." This aspect of delivery implies that we must move away from blanket statements. What has surfaced in the research about timing is that general statements are often not received and integrated because almost everyone listening believes we are not talking to them (Hattie & Clarke, 2019).

Take a look at these examples. Again, put a check by those that are just-in-time and just-for-me.

1. "Everyone needs to check and make sure you have your verb tenses correct in your essay. I noticed a lot of you change tenses throughout your writing."

2. "Michael, I noticed at least six places where the verb tense changes in the essay."

3. "Folks, you are not using the meniscus to measure the volume of the solution."

4. "Sam, did you use the meniscus to find the volumes of those solutions? Can you show me how you made that measurement?"

5. "Thank you for submitting your position paper on the use of nuclear weapons. I will try to get you feedback in about two weeks."

6. "Before submitting your position papers, we are going to spend about 30 minutes in peer-to-peer feedback using the rubric for this task."

7. "As you finish your problem set, place your papers in the basket. I will have them graded by tomorrow."

8. "Today, you are going to practice solving single variable equations on IXL. This will make sure you get immediate feedback as you move through the problem set."

Again, the pattern continues. The even-numbered examples provided just-in-time and just-for-me feedback. However, we were tricky with these examples. You may have noticed that examples 6 and 8 involved feedback from someone/something other than the teacher. This is a teaser for upcoming modules. One of the ways we can feasibly offer just-in-time and just-for-me feedback is to "shift the lift." More on that later.

➡️ **Lastly, feedback should vary in terms of timing, amount, mode, and audience** (see Brookhart, 2008). We have unpacked this aspect of feedback delivery a bit more in the following chart. Take a look.

Feedback Strategies Can Vary in Terms of . . .	In These Ways . . .	Examples and Things to Consider
Timing	When is the feedback given? How often is the feedback given?	• Provide immediate feedback for content (right/wrong). • Delay feedback slightly for more mathematical practices and science and engineering practices. • Never delay feedback beyond when it would make a difference in students' learning in the moment. • Provide feedback as often as is practical for all processes, tasks, and products.
Amount	How many feedback points? How much information is in each point?	• Focus on those points that are directly related to the success criteria. • Choose those points that are essential for closing the gap. • Consider the developmental stage of the learner (e.g., kindergarteners compared to high school seniors).
Mode	Oral Written Visual/ demonstration	• Select the best mode for the message. • When possible, it is best to engage in dialogue and questioning with the learner. • Give written feedback on written work. • Use teacher or student modeling if "how to do something" is an issue or if the student needs an example.
Audience	Individual Group/class	• Individual feedback says, "The teacher values my learning." • Group/class feedback works if most of the learners need the feedback. If not, group/class feedback is not effective. • Would it suffice to make a comment when passing the learners as they work on a problem or experiment? • Is a one-on-one conference better for providing feedback?

Let's look at specific examples of each of the variables in feedback to begin to see how this is communicated in our schools and classrooms. We have developed several scenarios for you to consider. For each one, you decide which packaging or delivery of the feedback would lead to a greater possibility that the feedback would be received and integrated. Use the space in the third column to explain why you think so. Given that we have been together for 12 modules, be specific and draw from any of the ideas already unpacked in the previous modules.

Option 1	Option 2	Why?
An elementary teacher reads student writing samples and identifies common errors. She plans whole class instruction on the use of reasons to support opinions because nearly every student in the class has neglected to do so. She also plans small group lessons for students who had other errors in their writing, including tense, subject-verb agreement, or the lack of a clear opinion.	The teacher reads student work and provides written feedback to students. Students are expected to review the feedback and revise their papers accordingly.	
A history teacher uses an online game to quiz students. He displays a question and students select their response on their mobile phones. He then shows them the number of students who selected each option, asking them to talk with their partners about the data. He then invites students to respond to the question again before showing them the correct answer and asking them to discuss why the incorrect answers are not appropriate.	A history teacher gives a weekly quiz on Fridays, and students receive their results on Mondays. They take a cumulative test at the end of the unit.	

The key difference between each of the examples is the availability of timely feedback about the students' learning. Option 1 in each of the two examples suggests that the teacher was setting up the learning experience for learners to give and receive feedback at multiple points. These multiple points are derived from the establishing and sharing of clarity through learning intentions and success criteria. In other words, the teachers in Option 1 offered the opportunity to give and receive feedback as learners progressed from one success criterion to the next. Do you see how clarity plays a vital role in how feedback works?

Information about learners' performance within a specific timeframe allows them to use the information for adjusting their pathway forward. This supports where they should focus their time, energy, and effort. Without timely information, learners cannot know where to go next and often continue moving forward, even if they are going in the wrong direction.

Let's look at some more examples.

Option 1	Option 2	Why?
A teacher confers with students as they work on a problem-solving set of rational expressions. He asks individual students and pairs of students what they are working on. Listening to the students' thinking allows him to make a decision about how to respond in that moment. The teacher refers to his planned questions, anticipated student strategies, and the success criteria to choose his response.	A teacher collects a problem-solving set on rational expressions. He marks which answers are not correct and returns the problem-solving set to learners at the end of the week.	
A teacher marks the incorrect solutions in a problem-solving set on balancing equations and returns the set to learners at the end of the week. She asks them to partner up and identify where they made mistakes in each incorrect solution. They are to describe, in their own words, how they would solve the problem differently in the future.	A teacher returns a problem-solving set on balancing equations to learners at the end of the week. She informs the students that these problems will be on the final test and they should review this set prior to taking the test.	

These examples focus on timing, amount, mode, and audience. All four. However, we want to zero in on the decisions by these two teachers around the amount of feedback. Did you notice how the amount of feedback was limited, in both examples, to where the learners made their mistakes? Plus, the mode and audience were adjusted to allow for personalized feedback (i.e., just-for-me feedback). If the audience had been the whole group, how would feedback be received by learners that did not miss a particular type of problem? Odds are not well.

Now that you have reviewed ways to vary the time, amount, mode, and audience, let's build our toolkit for pulling this off in our own schools and classrooms. Identify several learning experiences that require the giving, receiving, and integrating of feedback. This could be a writing task, a science experiment, a classroom discussion, or anything you and your learners will do in an upcoming learning experience. Then, plan how you will give and receive feedback. We have provided space in the following pages, as well as an example to get you started.

Learning Experience: My learners have to solve equations using manipulatives.	
Timing	In addition to solving their equations using manipulatives, I am going to have them put their answers into IXL so they can immediately see if they found the correct answer.
Amount	I am going to focus on how they use the manipulatives to set up the problem and the decisions they make with the manipulatives. To avoid overwhelming them with feedback, I am not going to worry about them showing their steps on paper or which specific manipulatives they use.
Mode	Since this is a hands-on task, the feedback will be delivered orally and through modeling the task when there is a common error for the entire class.
Audience	In addition to feedback from me, they will be asked to stop at specific times during the class, share their problem-solving process with a neighbor, and give and receive feedback with that neighbor.

Learning Experience:	
Timing	
Amount	
Mode	
Audience	

Learning Experience:	
Timing	
Amount	
Mode	
Audience	

Learning Experience:	
Timing	
Amount	
Mode	
Audience	

(Continued)

(Continued)

Learning Experience:	
Timing	
Amount	
Mode	
Audience	

Again, the packaging matters. How we deliver the feedback plays a significant role in the feedback loop. Tuning in or tuning out has significant consequences on learning. Fortunately, there are a lot of ways we can package feedback. In fact, flip back to pages 149 and 150 in this module. Do you remember the examples that involved cues, technology, and peer feedback? Those are different ways to deliver feedback. The next several modules will explore how we can exchange task, process, and self-directed feedback using cues and reinforcements, technology, practice tests, and peer-to-peer feedback. If you are looking for ways to modify the timing, amount, mode, or audience, these same approaches help us do just that.

Before diving into the final four modules of this playbook, we want you to make one connection between this module and the feedback loop. In the space provided, scratch out an answer to the following reflective question: How do we use the three parts of the feedback loop to guide our decisions about timing, amount, mode, and audience?

How do we use the feedback loop (feed-up, feed-back, and feed-forward) in deciding the timing, amount, mode, and audience for feedback?

Take a moment to reflect on your learning. How are you progressing? Where do you need to spend a little more time in this module?

Consider these questions to guide your self-reflection and self-assessment:

1. Can I identify key components of communicating feedback?

2. Can I compare and contrast different ways to communicate feedback?

3. Can I analyze our own communication of feedback across these key components?

4. Can I relate the components of communicating feedback to the feedback loop?

Access videos and other resources at
resources.corwin.com/howfeedbackworks.

13

HOW DO CUES AND REINFORCEMENTS *COMMUNICATE* FEEDBACK?

LEARNING INTENTION

We are learning about the role of cues and reinforcements in communicating feedback.

SUCCESS CRITERIA

We have successfully completed this module when

1. We can describe what is meant by a cue and reinforcement.

2. We can generate examples of cues and reinforcements in our schools and classrooms.

3. We can explain the role of cues and reinforcements in supporting the feedback loop.

4. We can develop a plan for using cues and reinforcements to build learners' capacity to engage in self-regulation feedback.

Video 13.1: Introduction to Module 13

resources.corwin.com/ howfeedbackworks

Feedback can be communicated through cues and reinforcements. Cues and reinforcements take many forms in our schools and classrooms. In this module, we want to

→ Define what is meant by a cue and reinforcement,

→ Compare and contrast these two approaches to communicating feedback, and

→ Describe how to implement these in our schools and classrooms.

Return to Module 2 or revisit www.visiblelearningmetax.com. Locate the effect size for cues and reinforcements and place it below.

> Effect size for cues and reinforcements: _____
>
> Based on your understanding of effect sizes, how would you describe this effect size?

CUES

Learning or instructional cues are those things in a learning environment that prompt learners about where to go next. These cues can be visual, verbal, kinesthetic, or environmental. As learners determine where they are going, how they are going, and where they are going next, any one of the four types of cues can prompt them. Let's look at a few examples.

>>> Examples of Visual Cues

1. As learners in Ms. Henry's class work on their narrative writing, Ms. Henry projects exemplars on the interactive board so that learners can visually see what makes a high-quality piece of writing. This gives them visual and immediate feedback on **where they are going.**

2. In marching band, Ms. Sorenson posts pictures of proper resting position and ready position with the different instruments around the band room. In fact, the pictures were co-constructed with her learners and her learners are the musicians featured in the pictures. If learners need feedback on either position during a performance, they can quickly look to see **how they are** supposed to be positioned for resting and ready positions.

3. As Ms. Fitzgerald's chemistry students finish their distillation lab in third-period chemistry, they are often uncertain about what to do with the waste from the laboratory. Proper disposal of chemicals is essential in science. Ms. Fitzgerald provides a laminated reference sheet at each laboratory station for learners to use in deciding **where to go next** with the chemical waste.

Look around your own school or classroom. What visual cues do you provide for your learners? List examples of visual cues in your learning environment and what feedback they provide to learners.

Examples of Verbal Cues

1. Ms. Berrang uses verbal cues in his elementary school gym class. To provide learners with feedback on overhand throwing, she uses the cues of *T, L, step and throw*. As learners begin to use overhand throwing to hit a target, the cues help them know **where they are going** in this psychomotor skill.

2. In mathematics, acronyms can be very helpful in simplifying expressions or solving equations. We have already referenced the order of operations in an earlier module. When learners use the acronym PEMDAS, they cue themselves in on **how they are doing** in simplifying an expression or solving an equation.

3. Let's look at a verbal cue that is focused on a behavioral outcome. In Ms. Berrang's gym class, ensuring learners have verbal cues about **where they are going next** in the gymnasium is essential for their safety. Ms. Berrang simply calls out, "1, 2, 3" and her learners stop what they are doing, face her, and put their hands on their knees. Oh, and they respond to her, "1, 2, 3, hands on my knees." This allows Ms. Berrang to provide the next set of instructions.

Reflect on your own school or classroom. What verbal cues do you provide for your learners? These can be behavioral, cognitive, affective, or emotional cues. List examples of verbal cues in your learning environment and what feedback they provide to learners.

>>> Examples of Kinesthetic Cues

1. Mr. Patterson uses kinesthetic cues to prompt learners about magnets. When he says the word "attracts," students bring their hands together with a loud clap. When he says the word "repel," students quickly pull their hands apart. This cues learners into **where they are going** in their study of charges and dipoles.

2. In world geography, learners have a song and dance that helps them know **how they are going** in identifying the continents, oceans, prime meridian, and the equator. No, we do not have a video of us singing this song, but you can see how this would help learners monitor their progress. During the test, Mr. McClure often observes his learners singing the song in their heads and quietly going through the motions at their desks.

3. Ms. Pizzulo is the athletic trainer at a local high school. She also teaches introductory courses in sports medicine at the Career and Technical Center. To get her learners to decide **where to go next** in evaluating a wrist injury, common in basketball, she relates the movements of pronation and supination using gestures: "When an athlete supinates, it looks like they are holding a bowl of soup, which is the beginning sound of the word *supination*."

Whether a song and dance or gesture, we all use kinesthetic cues in our classrooms. List some examples of kinesthetic cues in your learning environment and what feedback they provide to learners.

>>> Examples of Environmental Cues

1. In Ms. Williams' language arts classroom, learners move between multiple stations based on their specific goals and tasks for the day. To support learners in **knowing where they are going** in their learning, she has the room set up to reflect different goals and tasks. In the back corner, beanbags are spaced out, the lighting is soft, and there are posters on the wall about active reading. That is the silent reading section. Then there are tables with pencils, erasers, paper, and laptops. This is the writing center. There is another table with chairs for conferencing.

2. Ms. King has her biology room divided into two parts: the classroom space and the laboratory space. The laboratory space has lab coats, goggles, and emergency eyewash stations. Learners know that if they cross into that space, they should **check to ensure** they have all the necessary and required safety equipment with them (e.g., **how they are going**).

3. One more behavioral example: when the time comes for Ms. Anderson's first graders to transition to specials, all she has to do is walk over to the door and turn off the lights. Learners spring into action, cleaning up their workspace, putting supplies away, and efficiently moving to the door. The simple change in lighting cues them **where to go next**.

How do you use your classroom environment to cue learners? What are these environmental cues? While behavioral cues are the easiest to recall, try to identify cognitive, affective, or emotional cues. List examples of environmental cues in your learning environment and what feedback they provide to learners.

What makes cues so powerful in how feedback works is their support in answering the three questions associated with effective feedback:

Where am I going?

How am I going?

Where do I go next?

Whether these cues are acronyms, alliteration, rhymes, similes, slogans, dances, or specific locations in your classroom, they provide immediate and accessible feedback to learners. This feedback helps them adjust where they focus their attention, what they should devote their cognitive resources to, and how to retain the essential content, skills, and understandings.

Cues help learners and communicate feedback in three ways:

1. **Attend to specific content, skills, and understandings.** The feedback to the learners is communicated as "focus here, not there."

2. **Make meaning of ideas, concepts, and skills.** The feedback to learners is communicated as "think of it this way, not that way."

3. **Retain essential information.** The feedback to learners is communicated as "remember this, above and beyond that."

But wait—you will notice that the examples for each of the four types of cues involve the teacher giving feedback to learners. As we have emphasized throughout this entire playbook, feedback is often given by the learners to the teacher. In the chart below, flip this around. What cues could you explicitly teach to your learners so that they can prompt you during the learning experience about where you are going, how you are going, and where you should go next?

We got you started with an example.

Cue	What will this cue communicate to me or the learners?
The ASL sign for "I agree" **Image source:** iStock.com/OvsiankaStudio	For the students, this lets them know who agrees with their particular claim or statement. For me, this allows me to see where other learners are in their thinking.

(Continued)

Cue	What will this cue communicate to me or the learners?

What cues could you explicitly teach to your learners so that they can prompt *you*?

Notice the nature of your challenges and those aspects of each cue that might limit the impact of the feedback loop. For example, simply giving the ASL sign for "I agree" is not enough feedback from your learners about where they are in their thinking. Likewise, learners seeing that their classmates agree with their thinking does not clarify what about the thinking they agree with. All of it? Some of it? Cues must be followed-up and verified with additional opportunities to make thinking and learning visible. For example, after using the ASL "I agree" cue, what could you follow up with to verify that particular cue? For ideas, return to Module 9. List your ideas in the space on the next page.

CUES AND NOTICING

We need to address two more aspects of cues for feedback. The first of these aspects is the relationship between cues and noticing. Having visual, verbal, kinesthetic, and environmental cues is one thing. Ensuring that we and our learners notice those cues and then integrate those cues into where we are going next is something different. Take, for example, the visual cue for the area model of multiplication. We want learners to go from the first picture to the second picture. Receive the cue and then integrate the cue into their problem solving.

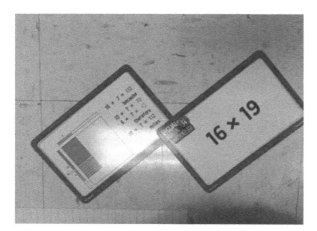

Even with this visual cue on the back of the problem card, some learners may not flip the card over to receive and integrate the visual cue. Some learners may flip the card over and receive the visual cue but not integrate the cue into their next steps.

How do we get learners to take the next steps in integrating the cues into their learning? When cues are introduced in our schools or classrooms, they should never be used in isolation. Returning to our example with the area model of multiplication, this cue must be introduced in steps and accompanied by other cues. Ms. Booth introduces this cue by modeling the process (kinesthetic cues) and using verbal cues to show learners how to set up the problem. Over time, she no longer has to verbally cue them about the problem.

Return to your examples of visual, verbal, kinesthetic, and environmental cues on pages 160–162 of this module. What would be your process for implementing these particular cues in your classroom? Remember to use your examples, not ours. We want this to be something you can put into use as soon as possible. We have taken our example from earlier and continued to use it as an example.

For now, leave that last column blank. We will return to that column at the end of the module.

Cue	What this cue will communicate to me or the learners?	What is the process for putting this into practice in your classroom?	
Visual Cues			
The ASL sign for "I agree" **Image source:** iStock.com/OvsiankaStudio	For the students, this lets them know who agrees with their particular claim or statement. For me, this allows me to see where other learners are in their thinking.	**Process:** 1. Introduce and model the sign. 2. For the first few days, I will need to prompt learners to use this sign instead of blurting out.	**Task:** **Process:** **Self-Regulation:**

Cue	What this cue will communicate to me or the learners?	What is the process for putting this into practice in your classroom?	
Verbal Cues			
		Process:	Task: Process: Self-Regulation:
Kinesthetic Cues			
		Process:	Task: Process: Self-Regulation:
Environmental			
		Process:	Task: Process: Self-Regulation:

The process of introducing cues into your classroom draws from the research on noticing. Remember, noticing involves three things. Return to Module 10, page 124, and list them here:

1.

2.

3.

The same three aspects of noticing apply here. We must support learners in noticing the cues, making meaning of the cues, and then integrating the cues into their next steps. The same goes for us. We have to recognize the cues of our learners, make meaning of those cues, and then integrate them into our next steps.

UNINTENTIONAL CUES

We have to recognize the cues of our learners, make meaning of those cues, and then integrate them into our next steps.

We would be remiss if we did not mention that some cues are *not* planned. Yes, our learners are giving and receiving cues simply by being present in our classroom and interacting with us and their classmates. Learners may cue us in through their body language, asking questions, fidgeting in their seats, or their movement in the room. What is happening when learners drop their shoulders, ask why they have to know something, begin to squirm in their seats, or avoid interacting with their group? For us, what cues are we sending when we cross our arms, change the tone of our voice, ask demanding questions, or move toward a particular desk or student?

Ensuring that the giving, receiving, and integrating of feedback moves teaching and learning forward, we have to be aware of unintentional cues that could distract from that goal.

Reflect on the unintentional cues you give and receive from learners. What can you do to recognize those cues and integrate them into where to next in teaching and learning? We have provided an example to get you started.

Example:

1. I need to be careful that my voice tone does not cue learners that I am mad at them or don't believe they can do it.

2. I need to notice when my learners are giving me a cue that they need a break or are not following me.

3.

As we close out this module, we need to address reinforcements. If you recall, this module was all about cues and reinforcements. However, all our time has been devoted to cues. There is an interesting and powerful connection between these two ways of communicating feedback. Get ready. This next part is very important.

Cues prompt learners about where to go next in their learning. Reinforcements signal if they successfully received and integrated those cues.

Another way to think about this interesting and powerful connection is this: cues get us going, and reinforcements tell us if we are going in the right direction.

> **Reinforcements signal if students successfully received and integrated our cues.**

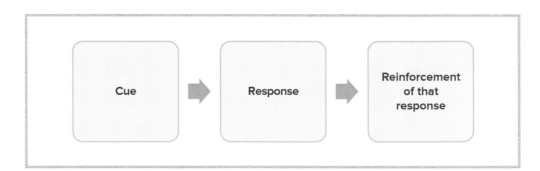

Reinforcements come in the form of task, process, or self-regulation feedback. Yep, the very content from Module 11. Take a minute to flip back to that module. Review the characteristics and differences between task feedback, process feedback, and self-regulation feedback. You are going to apply that learning to this module as a closing task.

Return to the chart on page 166 of this module. Remember, we were to leave the last column blank. Now we get to go back and use that last column. That last column is for reinforcing the cue. Take the remaining time in this module and provide examples of task, process, and self-regulation feedback you would use or see that would reinforce the responses to cues. Here is an example.

Cue	What this cue will communicate to me or the learners?	What is the process for putting this into practice in your classroom?	
Visual Cues			
The ASL sign for "I agree"  **Image source:** iStock .com/OvsiankaStudio	For the students, this lets them know who agrees with their particular claim or statement. For me, this allows me to see where other learners are in their thinking.	**Process:** 1. Introduce and model the sign. 2. For the first few days, I will need to prompt learners to use this sign instead of blurting out.	**Task:** Michael, remember, we are not blurting out. Use the sign we have for "I agree." Giovanni, thank you for using the sign we have for "I agree." **Process:** Everyone, how do we let someone know that we agree with their claim or statement? Josephine, do you agree with Giovanni's statement? **Self-Regulation:** From a student: "Ms. Bradley, I forgot the sign I am supposed to use." A learner looks over at his neighbor for a reminder of the sign for "I agree."

From cues and reinforcements, let's move to communicating feedback with technology.

Take a moment to reflect on your learning. How are you progressing? Where do you need to spend a little more time in this module?

Consider these questions to guide your self-reflection and self-assessment:

1. Can I describe what is meant by a cue and reinforcement?

2. Can I generate examples of cues and reinforcements in our schools and classrooms?

3. Can I explain the role of cues and reinforcements in supporting the feedback loop?

4. Can I develop a plan for using cues and reinforcements to build learners' capacity to engage in self-regulation feedback?

online resources

Access videos and other resources at
resources.corwin.com/howfeedbackworks.

14

HOW CAN TECHNOLOGY *COMMUNICATE* FEEDBACK?

LEARNING INTENTION

We are learning about the role of technology in communicating feedback.

SUCCESS CRITERIA

We have successfully completed this module when

1. We can explain what is meant by "shift the lift."

2. We can identify examples of when technology is an appropriate means for communicating feedback and when it is not appropriate.

3. We can explain the role of technology in supporting the feedback loop.

4. We can develop a plan for using technology to build learners' capacity to engage in self-regulation feedback.

Return to Module 2 or revisit www.visiblelearningmetax.com. Locate the effect size for feedback with technology and place it on the next page.

Video 14.1: Introduction to Module 14

resources.corwin.com/ howfeedbackworks

Effect size for feedback with technology: _____

Based on your understanding of effect sizes, how would you describe this effect size?

The wide range of instructional technologies is correlated with the wide range of ways those technologies support the exchange of feedback in our schools and classrooms. While instructional technology alone is not the key to effective teaching and learning, advances in this area have offered us a wider palette of tools to create a dynamic, engaging, and enriching learning experience for our students. The same can be said for feedback.

Return to the introduction of this playbook. We highlighted four questions that commonly come up in discussions about giving, receiving, and integrating feedback into our classrooms. We want to return to the first two of those questions now.

1. When we have a full classroom of students and a variety of assignments and tasks, how can we possibly ensure that all of them get the feedback they need?

2. What type of feedback is most helpful in learning? Simply telling students that a particular response or action is not correct cannot be enough, right?

3. How do we get our students to receive the feedback and edit, revise, or change their approach the next time? What if our students simply toss the feedback in the book, desk, backpack, or, even worse, the trashcan?

4. What role do our students play in giving and receiving feedback? After all, they will not be in our classrooms forever and will have to transition to independent learners.

Technology allows us to "shift the lift" in communicating feedback.

When we have a room full of learners, how can we possibly communicate the feedback that each learner needs within the time frame that this feedback is most helpful? Technology can help us here. What about different modalities for giving that feedback? Technology can help us here. Technology allows us to "shift the lift" in communicating feedback.

Shifting the lift means using available resources to alleviate the pressure solely falling on our shoulders.

If you do the math, ensuring that every learner in our classroom gets regular feedback takes time. Determining whether learners need task or process takes time. Monitoring their self-regulation feedback takes time. We do not want to leave you overwhelmed or feel overwhelmed ourselves. The research on feedback with technology offers us options that allow us to make more efficient use of our time.

Let's look at the four practices for communicating feedback. For cues and reinforcements, you can return to the previous module to help complete the below chart. For the other three practices, make some predictions about the role of the practice in "shifting the lift." We provided an example to get you started.

Practices for Communicating Feedback	How does this practice help shift the lift?
Cues and reinforcements	By placing an anchor chart of active reading marks; learners can refer to the chart or I can simply point them to the chart. This offers them an opportunity to engage in self-regulation feedback and allows me to devote time to other learners needing more scaffolded or personalized feedback.
Technology	
Practice tests	
Peer feedback	

Now let's move to the role of technology. What technologies do you have access to in your school or classroom? Generate a list. Don't leave something off the list if, at first glance, it does not seem to be helpful in communicating feedback.

We will come back to that list throughout the remainder of the module. For now, we want to provide some examples of what this looks like in classrooms.

TECHNOLOGY AND THE DIFFERENT TYPES OF FEEDBACK

With the development of online questioning platforms (e.g., IXL, Achieve3000), learners can engage in question sets and problem-solving sets that provide them with immediate feedback on the accuracy of their responses. Furthermore, we can adjust the level of complexity and difficulty, as well as identify the specific content and skills that will be practiced in a particular experience. For example, if language arts teachers need to adjust the text in a text-based questioning exercise, they have that option. If mathematics teachers need some learners to work on equations involving decimals while others only work with whole numbers, they have that option. We can make so many adjustments to what learners actually see and do on these platforms that we can ensure the feedback is directed toward areas of growth.

> The type of feedback described above is _____.

In addition to task feedback, technology can support the giving, receiving, and integrating of process feedback. Take a moment to return to the definition of process feedback on page 139 in Module 11. Make sure you are clear on what is meant by process feedback and how process feedback is different from the other three types.

Develop your own summary of process feedback. Provide some examples.

Now, let's do something with this summary of process feedback. We are going to ask you to apply this summary to your list of instructional technologies on page 174 of this module to giving, receiving, and generating process feedback. You will notice that the list of examples of process feedback is the same list we provided in Module 11. This time, we want you to generate several ideas about different technologies that would support the exchange of process feedback. We did the first one for you as an example.

Examples of Process Feedback	How would technology support the exchanging of this feedback?
"Joey, why is it important that we balance the chemical equations? What role do the coefficients play in understanding why some reactions are limited?"	I could provide a worked example using Loom that provides the narrated process. Learners could use the Loom file to stop and check their process using the process-based questioning.
"What do you notice about this painting and the decisions the artist appears to have made in creating this piece of art? What does this remind you of in today's world?"	
"If you and I get different answers when we simplify the same expression, how do we know which one is correct? What might help ensure that we arrive at the same answer?"	
"What is the rhyming scheme of this poem? How does that help you understand the context of the poem? What information is communicated through that rhyming scheme?"	
"How is this problem different from the previous problem? Did you treat the inequality sign the same in both problems?"	

Technology can support how we communicate self-regulation feedback.

Fill in the missing words.

Self-regulation feedback refers to learners' ability to _____ _____ _____ _____ when they approach a new and different problem, are stuck, or have to apply their understanding in a new way. When we have reached a _____ _____ of _____ _____ and are armed with multiple strategies or processes, we are ready to self-regulate our own feedback.

Return to the definition of self-regulation feedback on page 141 in Module 11. Make sure you are clear on what is meant by process feedback and how process feedback is different from the other three types.

What are the characteristics of your learners that tell you they are ready for self-regulation feedback? In other words, what are your look-fors? This is important for the effective use of technology in giving, receiving, and integrating self-regulation feedback.

Again, we are going to ask you to apply this list of look-fors to your list of instructional technologies on page 174 of this module to giving, receiving, and generating self-regulation feedback. You will notice the list of examples from self-regulation feedback is the same list we provided in Module 11. Just as you did with the process feedback examples, generate several ideas about different technologies that would support the exchange of self-regulation feedback. We did the first one for you as an example.

Examples of Self-Regulation Feedback	How would technology support the exchanging of this feedback?
The teacher overhears Joey say, "Wait a minute. The law of conservation of mass says we cannot have more atoms on one side than we have on the other. Something is wrong. We have to go back and check our coefficients and subscripts."	Learners would have access to the online resources associated with their textbooks. When recognizing the need for more feedback, they would utilize those tools to engage in self-directed study of examples to revise their own work.
A student in art history shares, "These paintings look very similar in style. But they cannot be from the same artist. What were the key features for pointillism again? That is where we need to start."	
A math teacher observes that several students are stuck on multiple problems in this week's independent practice work. However, she notices that Alfonzo has grabbed his interactive math notebook and is working through the examples again. He is actually placing the examples next to the problem set and comparing and contrasting them.	
As her English 12 students begin their independent analysis of a poem, the teacher watches several of them use the lettering technique she taught them to identify the rhyming scheme for each poem.	
Before turning in today's exit ticket, Isabella goes over each inequality and checks her decision making. Prior to today's class, she developed a step-by-step process from her notes that she uses to double-check her work.	

Before we move to the final tasks of this module, we want to offer some suggestions for using technology to communicate feedback. Some of these ideas you may be very familiar with in your classroom. Others may offer a new way of thinking about shifting the lift and using technology.

 ## Interactive Videos

Interactive videos (e.g., PlayPosit, EdPuzzle), whether teacher made or commercially produced, require students to respond to questions interspersed throughout the video. Interactive techniques like this are commonly done in face-to-face teaching, such as using interactive read-alouds that are punctuated with questions intended to foster comprehension. However, interactive videos offer a superior advantage that cannot be fully replicated in live teaching: The student has full control over the video and can view the video as often and as many times as needed. This allows learners to rewatch segments that are more difficult or complex.

How can you use interactive videos and the associated questions to support the giving, receiving, and integrating of feedback? Be specific to your classroom and content area.

 ## Intelligent Tutoring Systems

Intelligent tutoring systems (ITS) are commercially produced and mirror many of the best features of feedback. Information is presented, and the system asks questions, provides feedback or hints, and gives prompts. Based on the student's responses, the system adapts questions, feedback, and prompts (Ma et al., 2014). Examples of ITS programs include AutoTutor, Cognitive Tutor, and ALEKS. It should be noted that ITS programs are not "plug and play" and require investment in professional learning for teachers.

How can you use intelligent tutoring systems to support the giving, receiving, and integrating of feedback? Be specific to your classroom and content area.

Digital Exit Slips

Provide students with a range of possible responses and ask them to use the options at the end of learning experiences using Google Forms, Kahoot!, or some other online platform. With virtual exit slips, students are offered four possible responses to choose from:

1. I'm just learning. (I need more help.)

2. I'm almost there. (I need more practice.)

3. I own it! (I can work independently.)

4. I'm a pro! (I can teach others.)

The key to successfully implementing virtual exit slips lies in their direct connection to the learning experience, success criteria, or both. Based on the learners' responses, we can set up tomorrow's groups to address specific needs or provide opportunities for enrichment. In addition, we have vital information that allows us to see how accurately they are assessing their own learning.

How can you use virtual exit slips to support the giving, receiving, and integrating of feedback? Be specific to your classroom and content area.

>>> Digital Retellings

Retellings are used with elementary students for a variety of purposes, including fostering listening comprehension, oral composition, sequencing ability, attention, and memory. For younger children, retellings allow teachers to determine whether a child can process language when the burden of reading a text is removed. One of the easiest ways to do this is to read a short text to a student and then invite them to retell the story. Paired with a rubric for retelling informational and narrative texts, both we and our learners can exchange feedback on how they are progressing with their listening comprehension, oral composition, sequencing ability, attention, and memory.

How can you use retellings to support the giving, receiving, and integrating of feedback? Be specific to your classroom and content area.

>>> Polling to Respond to Questions

We can use polls to solicit information from students in our classroom. Whether responding with their mobile phones or clickers, learners can communicate about specific content, skills, and understandings during the learning experience. With almost all polling platforms, a bar graph populates on the shared screen to gauge the number of correct and incorrect responses. Similar polling functions are often built into learning management systems and provide feedback to the teacher in real time about the current learning progress.

How can you use polling to support the giving, receiving, and integrating of feedback? Be specific to your classroom and content area.

As we wind down this module, we have a big ask for you. While technology is incredibly helpful at communicating task, process, and self-directed feedback, the instructional tools we have at our fingertips can also help ensure that we have the right timing, mode, amount, and audience with that feedback. Take a glance at Module 11 to ensure you recall what we mean by each of these characteristics of feedback. Then, with technology on your mind, complete the below chart that asks you to tie this all together.

As always, we have provided several examples to get you started.

	Timing	Amount	Mode	Audience
Task feedback		**By using interactive tutoring systems, task feedback can be based on the specific question or problem, not the whole concept or topic.**		
Process feedback				**Using Google Docs, I can ensure that only those that need this particular feedback get it.**
Self-regulation			**Some learners prefer to read, while others prefer to listen to information or view an image. Technology allows me to offer those options.**	

And now we are on to practice testing.

Take a moment to reflect on your learning. How are you progressing? Where do you need to spend a little more time in this module?

Consider these questions to guide your self-reflection and self-assessment:

1. Can I explain what is meant by "shift the lift"?

2. Can I identify examples of when technology is an appropriate means for communicating feedback and when it is not appropriate?

3. Can I explain the role of technology in supporting the feedback loop?

4. Can I develop a plan for using technology to build learners' capacity to engage in self-regulation feedback?

Access videos and other resources at
resources.corwin.com/howfeedbackworks.

15

HOW DO PRACTICE TESTS *COMMUNICATE* FEEDBACK?

We are learning about the role of practice tests in communicating feedback.

SUCCESS CRITERIA

We have successfully completed this module when

1. We can explain what is meant by practice testing.

2. We can describe the process for using practice testing to engage in the feedback loop.

3. We can explain the role of practice testing in the active retrieval of content, skills, and understandings.

4. We can develop a plan for using practice testing to amplify the giving, receiving, and integrating of feedback in our schools and classrooms.

Video 15.1: Introduction to Module 15

resources.corwin.com/ howfeedbackworks

The opportunity to engage in practice testing allows both us and our learners to clearly see additional opportunities for learning. The underlying belief that makes practice testing so powerful is a belief we mentioned at the very beginning of our journey through this playbook.

Return to page 41 in Module 4. The fourth statement is the key belief behind the role of practice tests in communicating feedback. Please rewrite that statement here:

Let's look at this idea from a different perspective. If learners do not make mistakes, then what is the role of feedback? The power of feedback, the beauty in how feedback works, comes from mistakes. Mistakes are to feedback like sound is to a musician. Without sound, musicians never know the impact of their music. Without mistakes, we never know the impact of teaching on student learning.

Return to Module 2 or revisit www.visiblelearningmetax.com. Locate the effect size for practice tests and place it here.

Effect size for practice tests/testing effect/testing: _____

Based on your understanding of effect sizes, how would you describe this effect size?

We will admit, right up front, that practice testing as a means for communicating feedback is a bit surprising. Actually, anything with the word "test" in it seems to be the antithesis of what we have unpacked in this playbook. In our minds and the minds of our learners, practice tests are not any different from regular tests and tests of any kind of equal grades. Not just any grades, grades that matter. Grades that sting. Grades that are internalized as part of our identity.

What happens when you hand back a practice test to your learners? How do learners respond if they earn what they would classify as a "good grade"? How do learners respond if they earn a "not-so-good grade"?

Take a moment to explain why practice tests do not seem like a viable way to communicate feedback. (Hint: Revisit the feedback loop, the three questions, or the different types of feedback.)

A complicating factor behind practice tests is that research strongly indicates that the act of taking a test improves learning. So, here we are in Module 15 and we are going to add one more layer of complexity to how feedback works. However, we are going to address this additional layer in this module.

The Dilemma

Actively retrieving information increases the retention of content, skills, and understandings.

Practice tests ask learners to actively retrieve content, skills, and understandings.

But practice tests, or anything with the word "test" in it, create anxiety.

To address this dilemma, let's tackle each of these three statements in order.

ACTIVELY RETRIEVING INFORMATION INCREASES THE RETENTION OF CONTENT, SKILLS, AND UNDERSTANDINGS

Any time we "go and get" content, skills, or understandings from previous knowledge, we are engaged in active retrieval. You may now recognize many of the tasks throughout this playbook are active retrieval tasks. Over and over again, we have asked you to return to a particular module or a particular page and retrieve some concept, idea, or term. We have also asked you to retrieve experiences and examples from your own school or classroom that represent the concept, idea, or term with that particular module. This is active retrieval. Once we learn something the first time, the act of retrieval is the reactivation of that learning through active processing. The act of "going and getting" information is well-documented in the research as a means for moving learning forward (see Bjork, 1975; Roediger & Karpicke, 2006). Rather than insist that you review this research, we have selected the major findings on active retrieving in teaching and learning.

> **Any time we "go and get" content, skills, or understandings from previous knowledge, we are engaged in active retrieval.**

1. The act of retrieval is a memory modifier. Whatever information is retrieved becomes strengthened.

2. Instead of repeated restudying, learners are far better off testing themselves, both early and often.

3. This does not mean that we administer more tests, but rather provide numerous opportunities for students to retrieve previously learned information from memory.

4. With feedback, either by seeing the answers or reviewing the information, the benefits of testing become even more powerful.

5. When material is studied over several sessions and tested in a new context, varying the contexts of study results in better performance.

So how do these findings apply to our schools and classrooms? In the chart that follows, explain how you might translate these findings into your learning experiences. Then, in the third column, link the foundational elements of feedback to the research on retrieval after revisiting page 45 in Module 4. Remember, there may be more than one foundational element per research finding.

Research Finding About Retrieval	Possible Application to My Classroom	Connection to the Foundational Elements of Feedback
Learners are far better off **testing themselves,** both early and often.		
Provide learners with **numerous opportunities** to retrieve previously learned information from memory.		
Mistakes are okay! **When learners make mistakes, receive feedback, and have the opportunity to revise the information,** the benefits of retrieval are enhanced.		
Varying the context of retrieval enhances the benefit as well.		

PRACTICE TESTS ASK LEARNERS TO ACTIVELY RETRIEVE CONTENT, SKILLS, AND UNDERSTANDINGS

Practice testing is any retrieval opportunity when learners respond to low-stakes practice questions about previously learned content, skills, or understandings. What separates practice testing, a highly effective learning strategy that is a means for communicating feedback, from other forms of testing (i.e., standardized tests or unit tests) is that

1. Practice testing is low stakes or no stakes

2. Practice testing is completed during the learning experience

3. Practice testing is something learners can engage in on their own or with peers

How is practice testing different from other tests in your school or classroom? Using the Venn diagram on the facing page, compare and contrast practice testing with other forms of testing across the four foundational elements of feedback.

You will notice the lines through the Venn diagram, each one representing a foundational element. This enhanced Venn diagram just asks you to compare and contrast practice tests and other tests around that specific feature or characteristic. Please use the Venn diagram to record your thinking or download the template from the resources page at resources.corwin.com/howfeedbackworks.

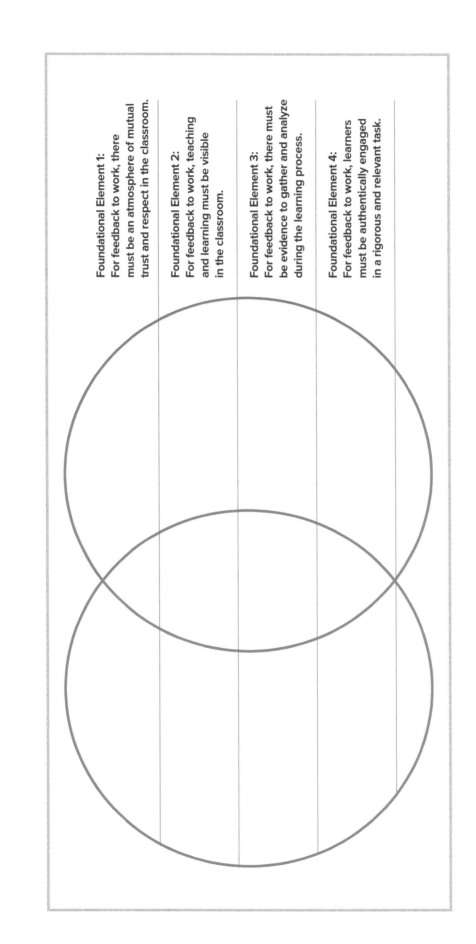

Foundational Element 1:
For feedback to work, there must be an atmosphere of mutual trust and respect in the classroom.

Foundational Element 2:
For feedback to work, teaching and learning must be visible in the classroom.

Foundational Element 3:
For feedback to work, there must be evidence to gather and analyze during the learning process.

Foundational Element 4:
For feedback to work, learners must be authentically engaged in a rigorous and relevant task.

Practice testing provides incredible benefits to both us and our learners. For example, practice tests are opportunities to generate evidence of student learning—making their current knowledge, skills, and understandings visible to us and them.

When learners generate responses to low-stakes practice questions, they are engaging in the retrieval of content, skills, and understandings. This benefit is enhanced when this practice testing is spaced out over time (e.g., a little now, a little later). Furthermore, when these low-stakes questions take on different forms (e.g., multiple-choice, free-response, or mixed responses), learners have the opportunity to access or retrieve their learning using different cues or prompts. Ah, yes, questions on practice tests can serve as a form of written or visual cues. For example, responding to a multiple-choice question requires a different kind of retrieval than a free-response question. However, in general, the benefits of practice testing are greater when learners must generate responses through free-response questions (Smith & Karpicke, 2014).

Using the chart provided, generate a list of all the different ways learners can engage in practice testing. Then, generate ideas about how you will use the practice test to enter into the feedback loop with learners. We have provided one example to get you started.

Examples of Practice Testing	How do you use the practice test to enter into the feedback loop?
During station work, Mr. Harouff's Algebra 1 students spend time completing a practice test using an online platform. Mr. Harouff can personalize the practice test based on where learners need additional practice. The students receive immediate feedback after each question and have the option of watching a video explanation of how to work on the specific problem.	**Feed-Up:** Before learners begin their practice testing, the computer platform provides an overview of the type of questions and the specific skill that each question is addressing. **Feed-Back:** Once learners respond to the question, they are given feedback on accuracy. Then, they are offered a video on the process for solving the problem. **Feed-Forward:** At the end of the practice test, learners get an analysis of their growth and areas for future opportunity (i.e., what they might want to practice more or engage in more learning).
	Feed-Up: **Feed-Back:** **Feed-Forward:**
	Feed-Up: **Feed-Back:** **Feed-Forward:**

Examples of Practice Testing	How do you use the practice test to enter into the feedback loop?
	Feed-Up: Feed-Back: Feed-Forward:
	Feed-Up: Feed-Back: Feed-Forward:

There is one more aspect of practice testing that we need to address. Practice testing should not come with a grade, but with feedback.

> **Practice testing *must* not be graded.**
>
> This is worth repeating a third time: **We should not link practice testing with a grade.**

Mistakes during practice testing are the conduits for giving, receiving, and integrating feedback in our schools and classrooms. For us, we get feedback on how learning is progressing that can guide our teaching decisions about where to go next. Our learners get self-feedback about where they are in their learning and where they need to devote time, effort, and energy.

Let's say that a sixth grader decides to engage in practice testing on reading comprehension. In their attempt to respond to both multiple-choice and free-response questions, the teacher and the learner notice several areas of opportunity for additional learning (i.e., the learner makes several mistakes and gets many of the questions wrong). Is this a problem? The answer: it depends. Whether making a mistake is beneficial or harmful depends on the learners' access to feedback (Butler & Roediger, 2008).

This feedback does not have to just come from us. This feedback can be a combination of feedback from technology (the previous module), feedback from peers (which we will address in the next module), feedback from us, and feedback from their own error analysis.

Connect cues and reinforcements with practice testing. What are some cues you could develop and use to support learners as they engage in practice testing?

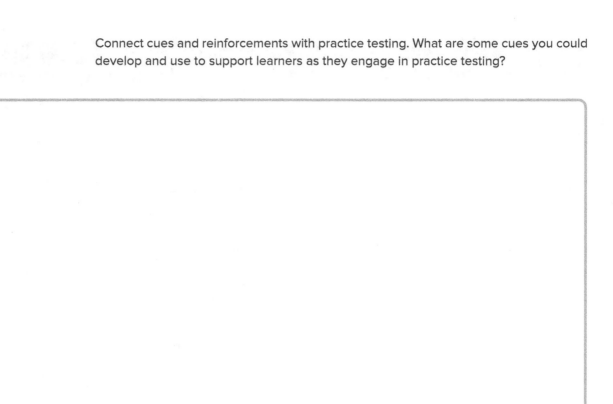

Ms. Fernandez teaches a foundation-in-mathematics course at the local middle school. She points out that "the content of this course can be very challenging to learners because they cannot always relate to the topics in mathematics. They often ask why they have to know something or if a certain problem is going to be on the test." As Ms. Fernandez tries to support her learners, she knows that they need to be a part of goal setting and progress monitoring and have choices in their learning experiences. "Plus, I know they need constant feedback to fuel their confidence in a subject that has historically given them trouble."

Ms. Fernandez found a way to tie clarity to their practice testing and error analysis. At the start of any unit, she previews the learning intentions and success criteria for the entire unit by providing them to the learners in a handout. "I need to get their feedback on where they think they are with particular mathematics concepts or problems." Her learners use their textbooks, laptops, and other classroom resources to decide where to place each success criterion on a quadrant that represents different levels of comfort.

SUCCESS CRITERIA QUADRANTS

I think I will find this hard.	I already know and can do this.

I need more explanation about this.	I need to spend more time on this.

This can also be done using presentation slides. A science teacher at the local high school creates a Google Slides deck containing the same quadrants (see page 193). She then generates text boxes that each contain a success criterion for the upcoming unit on erosion. Learners move the text boxes in and out of quadrants based on their level of comfort. Ms. Miller can monitor this from her own computer and engage learners when she needs evidence to support their self-assessment.

Ms. Fernandez and Ms. Miller do not stop there. Both teachers use a similar format to get feedback from their learners on practice tests and give feedback to learners. Ms. Fernandez shares that "after students complete a practice test, they either get immediate feedback from the computer or I provide them with feedback. But this feedback simply indicates whether the questions are correct or incorrect. Then, I provide them with an error analysis grid for them to complete."

Below is the error analysis grid used by both Ms. Fernandez and Ms. Miller. This process uses practice testing to give, receive, and integrate the feedback exchanged between the teachers and their learners.

ERROR ANALYSIS GRID

These are questions that I thought were hard that I got correct.	These are questions that I thought were easy that I got correct.
These are questions that I thought were hard that I got wrong. What is my next learning step?	**These are questions that I thought were easy that I got wrong. What is my next learning step?**

In both classrooms, the information communicated by these quadrants is integrated by Ms. Fernandez and Ms. Miller into their decisions about where to go next. The information communicated by these quadrants is integrated into learners' decisions about where to devote additional time, effort, and energy in their learning.

We have provided blank templates for both of these grids for you to use in your classroom. For a few minutes, brainstorm how you might use these quadrants.

We began this module with a dilemma.

The Dilemma

Actively retrieving information increases the retention of content, skills, and understandings.

Practice tests ask learners to actively retrieve content, skills, and understandings.

But practice tests, or anything with the word "test" in it, create anxiety.

The question now is, did we resolve this dilemma? We think so. The resolution of this dilemma lies in revising our view of practice testing. While, traditionally, any experience that has "test" in the title has been linked to finality or a grade, research says this is a very narrow view of testing, especially practice testing. Practice testing is another way to generate evidence that makes thinking and learning visible. When thinking and learning are visible, there is a valuable opportunity to give, receive, and integrate feedback. What we have unlocked in this module is that this opportunity assumes an active role for both us and our learners.

Briefly return to the previous module. Do you remember being asked to predict how the practices for communicating feedback would "shift the lift"? Go back and edit or revise your responses regarding practice tests. How do you now see practice testing as a way to shift the lift? Use a different color pen to make revisions so you can see the evolution of your thinking.

Before moving into the final module, flip back to page 191 in this module. Do you remember when we made a subtle reference to peer feedback? As it turns out, the exchange of feedback is quite powerful when given by peers. Let's talk about the role of peers in communicating feedback.

Take a moment to reflect on your learning. How are you progressing? Where do you need to spend a little more time in this module?

Consider these questions to guide your self-reflection and self-assessment:

1. Can I explain what is meant by practice testing?

2. Can I describe the process for using practice testing to engage in the feedback loop?

3. Can I explain the role of practice testing in the active retrieval of content, skills, and understandings?

4. Can I develop a plan for using practice testing to amplify the giving, receiving, and integrating of feedback in our schools and classrooms?

Access videos and other resources at
resources.corwin.com/howfeedbackworks.

16

HOW CAN WE ENGAGE OUR LEARNERS IN *COMMUNICATING* FEEDBACK?

LEARNING INTENTION

We are learning about peer feedback and how peer feedback improves the exchange of feedback in our schools and classrooms.

SUCCESS CRITERIA

We have successfully completed this module when

1. We can explain why peer feedback has such potential to improve learning.

2. We can explain the relationship between clarity and peer feedback.

3. We can identify the role of all Four Cs in ensuring peer feedback works.

4. We can develop a plan for building the skills necessary for learners to engage in peer feedback.

Return to Module 2 or revisit www.visiblelearningmetax.com. Locate the effect size for peer feedback and place it on the next page.

Video 16.1: Introduction to Module 16

resources.corwin.com/ howfeedbackworks

Effect size for peer feedback: _____

Based on your understanding of effect sizes, how would you describe this effect size?

We have saved what we believe to be the best for last. When learners take ownership of their learning and this ownership leads learners to hold each other accountable, we have reached the pinnacle of engagement. Let's visit the kindergarten classroom of Ms. Cornish and get a peek at this in action.

Ms. Cornish has intentionally partnered her learners up for a read-aloud task. In their pairs, students will take turns reading a text passage specifically selected for them to ensure the right level of challenge. When the pair decides who is going to read first, this student begins to read aloud to their partner. We will listen in to the conversation between Amelia and Jackson. After a quick conversation, Amelia decides that she will go first and read her passage to Jackson. Jackson does not get to sit and listen passively. Instead, he must follow along in the text and listen carefully to how Amelia is reading her text. Jackson has a rubric available to him that helps him notice the most essential parts of this read-aloud.

Fluency Rubric	4 Great	3 Good	2 Developing	1 Needs Practice
Speed Not too slow and not too fast.				
Accuracy Words skipped. Mistakes made.				
Expression Shows emotion. Sounds like a conversation.				
Flow Smooth. No robot reading.				

After some time, Amelia concludes her read-aloud and says to Jackson, "What feedback do you have for me?" Jackson refers to the rubric and shares his thoughts with Amelia. Jackson starts with speed by saying, "I thought you had nice speed. Not too slow and not too fast. I give you an 'awesome.'"

The kindergarteners giggle and Amelia thanks him for the feedback. He lets her know that there were a bunch of words that she skipped. "You found lots of words that you didn't know yet. But I bet the next time you will get it. So, I am going to give you a 2 so you can earn a 3 or 4 next time."

Jackson points out, "I like how you talked like the characters. That was funny and made me laugh. And you didn't sound like Alexa." Jackson concludes his feedback by coloring a 4 and the rest 3s.

They switch places and go through the process with Jackson reading and Amelia listening and providing feedback.

> Using a highlighter or colorful pen, go through the above example and highlight or underline things that jumped out at you in the example. Keep in mind that this example really happened. How it happens in our classrooms is the focus of this module.

Reviewing those things that jumped out at you in Ms. Cornish's classroom, make a list of the content, skills, and understandings that these learners had to have in their toolkits to successfully engage in peer feedback. In other words, what did you notice? Be specific!

Let us first be clear that peer feedback in this kindergarten class was fully implemented in March. However, from August to March, Ms. Cornish slowly introduced the content, skills, and understandings needed by her students to successfully give, receive, and integrate feedback with their peers. This was not accomplished overnight, nor was this accomplished by accident. As we examine and unpack Ms. Cornish's kindergarten classroom, she must build and sustain the Four Cs alongside her learners.

Take a second and retrieve the Four Cs for *how feedback works*. Next to each C, summarize what the C means in your classroom.

1.

2.

3.

4.

Ms. Cornish had to ensure that her learners

1. Are always fostering, nurturing, and sustaining positive and productive relationships among members of the classroom

2. Are working together to enhance each other's credibility by leveraging individual strengths during learning experiences

3. Have clarity about the shared learning intentions and success criteria for the learning experience where peer feedback is going to be offered

4. Have the cognitive, social, and affective skills to communicate with their peers

We have devoted a significant amount of time to learning about how we can lay the foundation for how feedback works. Implementing peer feedback requires the fusing together of everything in the first 15 modules and not just keeping this work for ourselves, but including our learners in this work as well.

When we build relationships in our classrooms, we should teach and support our learners to build relationships with their peers.

When we enhance our credibility in our classrooms, we should teach and support our learners to enhance credibility with their peers.

When we establish clarity in our classrooms, we should share that clarity and help learners find their own clarity in the learning.

When we seek to communicate feedback in our classrooms, we should increase it by allowing learners to communicate feedback to their peers.

We need to do some heavy lifting with these four callings to support peer feedback that works. You may need to flip back to early modules to review or retrieve information needed to complete the following chart.

In the first column, we have provided each of the Four Cs. We would like you to map out a plan for building the capacity in your learners so that they can give, receive, and integrate feedback among each other. We will get you started.

	What is needed to build this capacity in my students?
Care (relationships)	I need to create a culture of caring in my classroom; students acknowledge and respect each other's ideas; students recognize that we all learn at different rates.
Credibility	
Clarity	I need to make sure my students can answer the three clarity questions each and every day.
Communication	

For the rest of this module, we want to place an additional focus on two of the Cs: *clarity* and *communication*.

SHARING CLARITY FOR PEER FEEDBACK

As we build the capacity in our learners to give, receive, and integrate feedback between each other, we not only have to have clarity about the day's learning (e.g., the what, why, and how of the learning experience), we must show them what successful peer feedback looks like and sounds like when done well. Just as we can share learning intentions and success criteria related to fictional text, fractions, territorial expansion, or tropisms, we can share what successful peer feedback looks like during the learning experience.

The successful implementation of peer feedback requires care and credibility. This powerful process also requires us to show learners the target.

There is no one right way to share or communicate success criteria. There are at least seven different ways of sharing what success looks like with our learners:

1. **I Can Statements:** This form of success criteria is the most popular, but it may not always be the most effective means of implementation. "I can" statements are explicit and direct statements about what individual learners must do to demonstrate their learning. These statements also guide us in what to look for from individual learners.

2. **We Can Statements:** These explicit and direct statements take a collaborative view of learning. Rather than what individual learners must do, this form of success criteria highlights the value of collective learning and what learners and teachers are expected to do together.

3. **Single-Point Rubrics:** Rather than different levels of quality, a single-point rubric provides the expectations for mastery in a process, task, or product. In other words, only a single level of quality is provided for each expectation.

4. **Holistic/Analytic Rubrics:** Rubrics provide learners with the expectations for the process, task, or product, along with descriptions of the level of quality for each expectation.

5. **Teacher Modeling:** Helping learners understand expectations of success can come from us modeling the *content*, *practices*, and *dispositions*. This modeling allows learners to see success in action. Learners use the model to guide their own work toward the learning intention.

6. **Exemplars:** We can provide worked examples and/or exemplars of processes or finished tasks or products. Worked examples provide a comparison for learners to use in their own work, while exemplars possess all the expectations for success and can truly be a model for their learning path.

7. **Co-Constructing Criteria for Success:** The final way to implement success criteria is by co-constructing those expectations with learners. The process of co-constructing is a collaborative effort between teachers and students as they set the criteria for success before engaging in the work.

Below is a list of different approaches for sharing success criteria with learners. In the second column, develop a list of ways these approaches help learners give and receive feedback. In the third column, explain how these same approaches could show learners what successful peer feedback looks like in your classroom. We will provide some examples to get you started.

Approaches for Sharing Success Criteria	How do these approaches help learners give and receive feedback to each other?	How could these approaches be used to show what successful peer feedback looks like?
I can/We can statements		
Single-point rubrics	Learners can go down the items on the single-point rubric and give feedback based on those items.	
Holistic/analytic rubrics		
Exemplars		
Modeling		
Co-constructed success criteria		The teacher and learners could co-construct features of successful peer feedback that all members of the classroom are invested in during these opportunities.

The successful implementation of peer feedback requires care and credibility. This powerful process also requires us to show learners the target. If we want them to engage in peer feedback, we have to show them what this looks like. What we hope to have demonstrated here is that the same clarity that answers the what, why, and how of the day's learning can be used to clarify how to give, receive, and integrate feedback with their peers.

But there is one more aspect of peer feedback we would like to address: the language for communicating feedback.

THE LANGUAGE TO COMMUNICATE FEEDBACK

Disciplinary vocabulary includes those terms that are used in communicating about a particular content area. For example, *fauna and flora, quadrilaterals and hexagons, horizon line and perspective*, and *manifest destiny and jurisprudence* all represent terms that are linked to specific subjects. However, there is language that is used across subject areas and then language that is used in everyday life. Beck et al. (2013) describe these three types of vocabulary or language using a tiered system.

Tier 1 Vocabulary: These are words or terms that are used in everyday life and are common in spoken language. In many cases, this vocabulary is built through conversation. Examples of Tier 1 vocabulary include *notebook, book, happy, walk, animal, red, teacher, door, school,* and *room.*

Tier 2 Vocabulary: This cluster of terms is academic vocabulary that crosses multiple subject areas, for example, the processes of science (e.g., *predict, infer, analyze, evaluate*). Students need to know and understand these terms, as they will be part of their learning experience across all content areas and outside of the classroom.

Tier 3 Vocabulary: This set of words includes terms that are domain specific. This means that these terms mean something within the context of a discipline such as science, for example, and are key to understanding specific concepts in science. Examples of these words include *sound, vibrations, compressions, wavelength, frequency,* and *amplitude.*

For learners to successfully engage in peer feedback, they must have the necessary Tier 1, Tier 2, and Tier 3 vocabulary to communicate the feedback.

Ms. Cornish's learners use language to make progress in their own learning but must also use language to communicate feedback with each other. Amelia and Jackson had to have both content vocabulary (e.g., Tier 2 and Tier 3) and everyday life vocabulary (Tier 1) to clearly communicate in a way that is credible.

If you are considering using peer feedback in an upcoming learning experience or unit, what Tier 2 and Tier 3 vocabulary must be in place for this to be successful? List those terms in the following box. (Hint: If you have unpacked your standards, that will provide the Tier 2 and Tier 3 vocabulary.)

We must help learners develop this vocabulary and then use this vocabulary in classroom discussions, debates, and in the exchange of feedback. Oh, and when learners engage in these three actions, we receive feedback on how our teaching is moving student learning forward. That's right; when learners are giving each other feedback, we are getting feedback on how well we have implemented this process in our classroom.

Classrooms that successfully implement peer feedback are, and always have been, classrooms full of talk.

Let's return to Ms. Cornish's kindergarten classroom. For Amelia and Jackson to engage in such clear and credible talk, they must have had regular opportunities to develop this talk. Ms. Cornish's students do a lot of talking. Studies of teacher talk suggest that as much as 70 to 80 percent of instructional minutes are filled with the voice of the teacher, with the percentage increasing at higher grade levels (Sturm & Nelson, 1997). Student discourse is surprisingly rare even in content areas and grade levels where we might expect it to be common. True *discussion*, defined as academic exchanges between at least three people for at least 30 seconds, occurs rarely in secondary English classrooms, occupying less than 2 minutes per period (Wilkinson & Nelson, 2013). In other words, in many classrooms, teachers talk and students listen. That isn't a recipe for building the capacity for peer feedback.

Ms. Cornish not only has a classroom where students do a lot of talking, but she also uses cues and reinforcements to build the vocabulary that supports peer feedback. She uses anchor charts to provide sentence frames, sentence stems, and question starters that learners can use to communicate feedback with each other.

Classrooms that successfully implement peer feedback are, and always have been, classrooms full of talk.

ANCHOR CHARTS EXAMPLES

Giving	Receiving
I noticed that . . .	I appreciate you noticing that . . .
I wondered about . . .	I hadn't thought about that . . .
I was confused by . . .	I heard you say that _____ confused you.
I suggest that . . .	Based on your suggestion, I will . . .
Have you thought about . . .	Thank you. What would you do?
You might consider . . .	I'm not sure what that looks like. Tell me more.

Glow	Grow
I like how you . . .	It might be helpful to . . .
You did a wonderful/excellent/great job . . .	Perhaps you could . . .
You succeeded in . . .	Would it be better if I . . .
Terrific work on . . .	You may need more . . .
This is quality work because . . .	You may need less . . .
I like the way you included . . .	Your next steps might be . . .
I really enjoyed this because . . .	You might try . . .
I think the best thing about your work is . . .	Your response may be more effective if you . . .
The most outstanding aspect of your work is . . .	The task was to . . . Be sure to . . .

These are just two examples of anchor charts for building peer feedback vocabulary. You can design and present your own anchor charts. Better yet, co-construct these charts with your learners.

Peer feedback is an essential part of how feedback works for two main reasons. First, learners take feedback from their peers better than they take it from us. If our learners are going to give, receive, and integrate feedback between each other, we must make sure that feedback is accurate and truly moves learning forward.

Second, telling isn't teaching, and students cannot learn by listening alone. Giving feedback to their peers requires that they engage in noticing, retrieve content, skills, and understandings that they have already learned, and communicate in a way that makes sense to others. This improves learning.

The goal, then, of peer feedback is to provide abundant opportunities that transfer the use of academic language from the teacher to the students. In practice, this means being deliberate about when we use peer feedback, providing the scaffolding students need to build the skills for giving feedback to their peers, and then gradually releasing the responsibility to learners. This is exactly what Ms. Cornish did and why this process took until March to implement.

Briefly return to the previous module. Do you remember being asked to predict how the practices for communicating feedback would shift the lift? Go back to page 173 and edit or revise your responses regarding peer feedback. How do you now see peer feedback as a way to shift the lift? Use a different color pen to make revisions so you can see the evolution of your thinking.

As we have always done, take a look at the success criteria from the beginning of this module. Take a moment to reflect on your learning. How are you progressing? Where do you need to spend a little more time in this module?

Consider these questions to guide your self-reflection and self-assessment:

1. Can I explain why peer feedback has such potential to improve learning?

2. Can I explain the relationship between clarity and peer feedback?

3. Can I identify the role of all Four Cs in ensuring peer feedback works?

4. Can I develop a plan for building the skills necessary for learners to engage in peer feedback?

Access videos and other resources at
resources.corwin.com/howfeedbackworks.

Conclusion

After 16 modules, we have arrived at the end of this part of the journey. For us, this journey has been and will always be personal and professional. Each day, the three of us walk into our own schools and classrooms and interact with our colleagues and learners. The moment our feet cross the threshold of the doorway, we have one purpose: to have a measurable and positive impact on those we encounter. Those learners, those colleagues we see each and every day. We also know that they will have an impact on us. This impact extends beyond reading, writing, and arithmetic, into social and emotional learning as well. To have the type of impact we strive for every day, there must be feedback—feedback that works in moving learning forward.

What we hope to have accomplished over the past 16 modules is a deep dive into how that feedback works. Not just how feedback works in general, but how feedback works in your specific, unique, and powerful learning environment. We want to look back at the starting point of our journey. Below are the questions we posed in the introduction of this playbook.

1. When we have a full classroom of students and a variety of assignments and tasks, how can we possibly ensure that all of them get the feedback they need?

2. What type of feedback is most helpful in learning? Simply telling students that a particular response or action is not correct cannot be enough, right?

3. How do we get our students to receive the feedback and edit, revise, or change their approach the next time? What if our students simply toss the feedback in the book, desk, backpack, or, even worse, the trashcan?

4. What role do our students play in giving and receiving feedback? After all, they will not be in our classrooms forever and will have to transition to independent learners.

In the introduction, these were posed as concerns about feedback. How did we do in addressing these concerns? Take a moment to reflect on our learning journey. Do you have the beginnings of answers to these questions? We hope the answer is *yes*.

By now you have more than likely committed the effect size for feedback to memory, 0.62. This effect size does not represent a guarantee. No research offers a guarantee. What research offers us is evidence around specific approaches, interventions, and strategies that have the *potential* to influence the learning in your school or classroom. To move that research to reality or that potential to impact, we have to make adaptations to the specific approach, intervention, and strategy based on the local context of our classroom.

The feedback blockers in our classrooms will not look the same as the feedback blockers in your classroom. How we forge and sustain relationships and credibility depends on who is in our classroom. Since our learners will be different than your learners, that forging and sustaining will look different as well. This same logic applies to clarity and the communication of feedback as well. There is no "one-size-fits-all." That is exactly why the pages of this playbook shifted the lift to you. No one knows your students better than you do. How you blend the research and ideas in this playbook will be up to you—we just offered the ingredients.

What determines if your decisions resulted in the highest level of impact possible will depend on the evidence you generate and interpret each and every day. If the evidence says that your learners are farther along in their learning than they were when they arrived in your classroom, because of the feedback they gave, received, and integrated, then you made the best decision for that day.

Our journey together does not have to end with the conclusion of this playbook. We invite you to contact us. Share your experiences in making feedback work in your classroom. Share your successes, share examples, share your questions, and share the challenges that you encounter along the way. The odds are quite high that we will be walking the same journey as you as we strive to make feedback work in our classrooms.

As we close out this playbook, we want to solicit some feedback from you. Use the space below to answer the question we have been working on for the last 200 pages: *How does feedback work?*

Yes, the answer is complicated. But the time, effort, and energy we put into ensuring that feedback in our schools and classrooms works is worth it. This commitment makes sure that our learners have a great teacher, not by chance, but by design.

Thank you for learning alongside us. We are all better because of it.

References

Almarode, J., Fisher, D., Thunder, K., & Frey, N. (2021). *The success criteria playbook: A hands-on guide to making learning visible and measurable.* Corwin.

Almarode, J., & Vandas, K. (2013). *Clarity for learning: Five essential practices that empower students and teachers.* Corwin.

Beck, I. L., McKeown, M. G., & Kucan, L. (2013). *Bring words to life: Robust vocabulary instruction* (2nd ed.). Guilford Press.

Bjork, R. A. (1975). Retrieval as a memory modifier: An interpretation of negative recency and related phenomena. In R. L. Solso (Ed.), *Information processing and cognition: The Loyola symposium* (pp. 123–144). Lawrence Erlbaum.

Brookhart, S. (2008). *How to give effective feedback to your students.* Alexandria, VA: ASCD.

Brummelman, E., Thomase, S., Overbeek, G., Orobio de Castro, B., van den Hout, M. A., & Bushman, B. J. (2013). On feeding those hungry for praise: Person praise backfires in children with low self-esteem. *Journal of Experimental Psychology: General, 143*(1), 9–14. http://www.apa.org/pubs/journals/releases/xgeofp-brummelman.pdf

Butler, A. C., & Roediger, H. (2008). Feedback enhances the positive effects and reduces the negative effect of multiple-choice testing. *Memory & Cognition, 36*(3), 604–616.

Cornelius-White, J. (2007). Learner-centered teacher-student relationships are effective: A meta-analysis. *Review of Educational Research, 77*(1), 113–143.

Fendick, F. (1990). *The correlation between teacher clarity of communication and student achievement gain: A meta-analysis* [Doctoral dissertation]. University of Florida Digital Collections. https://ufdc.ufl.edu/AA00032787/00001

Finn, A. N., Schrodt, P., Witt, P. L., Elledge, N., Jernberg, K. A., & Larson, L. M. (2009). A meta-analytical review of teacher credibility and its associations with teacher behaviours and student outcomes. *Communication Education, 58*(4), 516–537. https://doi.org/10.1080/03634520903131154

Fisher, D., Frey, N., & Hattie, J. (2016). *Visible learning in literacy.* Corwin.

Fisher, D., Frey, N., Almarode, J., Flories, K., & Nagel, D. (2020). *The PLC+ playbook: A hands-on guide to collectively improving student learning, grades K–12.* Corwin.

Fisher, D., Frey, N., Amador, O., & Assof, J. (2018). *The teacher clarity playbook, grades K–12: A hands-on guide to creating learning intentions and success criteria for organized, effective instruction.* Corwin.

Hall, R. M., & Sandler, B. R. (1982). *The classroom climate: A chilly one for women?* Retrieved from https://files.eric.ed.gov/fulltext/ED215628.pdf

Hattie, J. (2009). *Visible learning: A synthesis of over 800 meta-analyses relating to achievement.* Routledge.

Hattie, J. (2012). *Visible learning for teachers: Maximizing impact on learning.* Routledge.

Hattie, J., & Clarke, S. (2019). *Visible learning feedback.* Routledge.

Hattie, J., & Timperley, H. (2007). The power of feedback. *Review of Educational Research, 77*(1), 81–112.

Hoy, W. K., & Tschannen-Moran, M. (1999). Five faces of trust: An empirical confirmation in urban elementary schools. *Journal of School Leadership, 9*(3), 184–208. https://doi.org/10.1177/105268469900900301

Jastrow, J. (1899). The mind's eye. *Popular Science Monthly, 54,* 299–312.

Ma, W., Adesope, O. O., Nesbit, J. C., & Liu, Q. (2014). Intelligent tutoring systems and learning outcomes: A meta-analysis. *Journal of Educational Psychology, 106*(4), 901–918.

Mehrabian, A. (1971). *Silent messages.* Wadsworth.

Merriam-Webster. (2021). Feedback. *Merriam-Webster.com.* https://www.merriam-webster.com/dictionary/feedback

Ritchhart, R., Church, M., & Morrison, K. (2011). *Making thinking visible. How to promote engagement, understanding, and independence for all learners.* Jossey-Bass.

Roediger, H. L., & Karpicke, J. D. (2006). The power of testing memory. Basic research and implications for educational practice. *Perspectives on Psychological Science, 1*(3), 181–210.

Schoenfeld, A. H. (2011). Noticing matters. A lot. Now what? In M. G. Sherin, V. R. Jacobs, & R. A. Philipp (Eds.), *Mathematics teacher noticing: Seeing through the teachers' eyes* (pp. 223–238). Routledge.

Sherin, M. G., Jacobs, V. R., & Philipp, R. A. (2011). Situating the study of teacher noticing. In M. G. Sherin, V. R. Jacobs, & R. A. Philipp (Eds.), *Mathematics teacher noticing: Seeing through the teachers' eyes* (pp. 3–13). Routledge.

Smith, M. A., & Karpicke, J. D. (2014). Retrieval practice with short-answer, multiple-choice, and hybrid tests. *Memory, 22*(7), 784–802.

Stone, D., & Heen, S. (2014). *Thanks for the feedback. The science and art of receiving feedback well*. Penguin.

Sturm, J. M., & Nelson, N. W. (1997). Formal classroom lessons: New perspectives on a familiar discourse event. *Language, Speech, and Hearing Services in Schools, 28*(3), 255–273. https://doi.org/10.1044 /0161-1461.2803.255

Visible Learning Meta[X]. (2022, January). https://www.visible learningmetax.com/

Wilkinson, I. A. G., & Nelson, K. (2013). Role of discussion in reading comprehension. In J. Hattie & E. Anderman (Eds.), *International guide to student achievement* (pp. 299–302). Routledge.

Index

CORWIN
A SAGE Publishing Company

Helping educators make the greatest impact

CORWIN HAS ONE MISSION: to enhance education through intentional professional learning.

We build long-term relationships with our authors, educators, clients, and associations who partner with us to develop and continuously improve the best evidence-based practices that establish and support lifelong learning.

CORWIN Fisher & Frey

> **Every student deserves a great teacher— not by chance, but by design.**

Read more from Fisher & Frey

Transform negative behavior into a teachable moment at your school, utilizing restorative practices that are grounded in relationships and a commitment to the well-being of others.

Rich with resources that support the process of parlaying scientific findings into classroom practice, this playbook offers all the moves teachers need to design learning experiences that work for all students.

Harnessing decades of Visible Learning® research, this easy-to-read, eye-opening guide details the six essential components of effective tutoring.

Catapult teachers beyond learning intentions to define clearly what success looks like for every student. This step-by-step playbook expands teacher understanding of how success criteria can be utilized to maximize student learning.

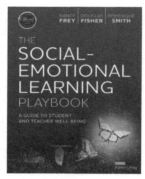

This interactive playbook provides the language, moves, and evidence-based advice you need to nurture social and emotional learning in yourself, your students, and your school.

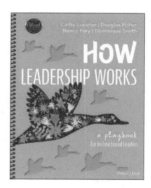

This easy-to-use playbook prompts educators to clarify, articulate, and actualize instructional leadership goals with the aim of delivering on the promise of equity and excellence for all.

To order your copies, visit corwin.com/FisherandFrey